My Underground *Everyday*

Over 100 inspiring recipes from Jess' Underground Kitchen

Written by Jess Daniell
Photos by Lottie Hedley

Ball
MASON

Ball
MASON

For my JUK dream team, who make magic every day

What does a chef eat when they cook at home?

Although I've never considered myself a 'chef', the type of food I cook reguarly at home changes as frequently as the seasons (or simply the day of the week!) There are times when I have so many fresh ideas and feel completely enamoured with creating new dishes. And there are also weeks where I lack motivation and fall into a food rut.

This is a book for all stages — simple and effective sauces and staples that will elevate your home cooking to the next level; innovative ways to utilise leftovers and get the most out of your meal prep; healthy everyday meals that are quick to whip together; plus a few aspirational dishes to keep your love of food glowing. I hunt out the freshest ingredients and eat with the seasons — crispy, light salads in summer and comforting curries and soups in the cooler months. That's what food is all about.

And for those nights when you simply can't fathom cooking... JUK does the hard work for you! Our ready-made meals are handmade in small batches with real ingredients, just like you would make at home. They're perfect for having on hand to pop in the oven, when you need something more nutritious and delicious than takeaways. Visit juk.co.nz to see what the team have been busy cooking this week.

Please use this book as a guide to help you on your own food journey — all recipes are my interpretation of flavours and combinations, ready and waiting for you to add your own flair.

A little insight and inspiration, from my home kitchen to yours...

Happy cooking!

Hello	6
Menu	9
Pickle Party	11
Saucy Staples	31
Breakfast Club	65
Snack Attack	89
Salad Bar	121
Everyday Meals	145
Heal Meals	171
Curry Night	195
Backyard BBQ	211
Festive Feast	229
Find it	260
Dream Team	267

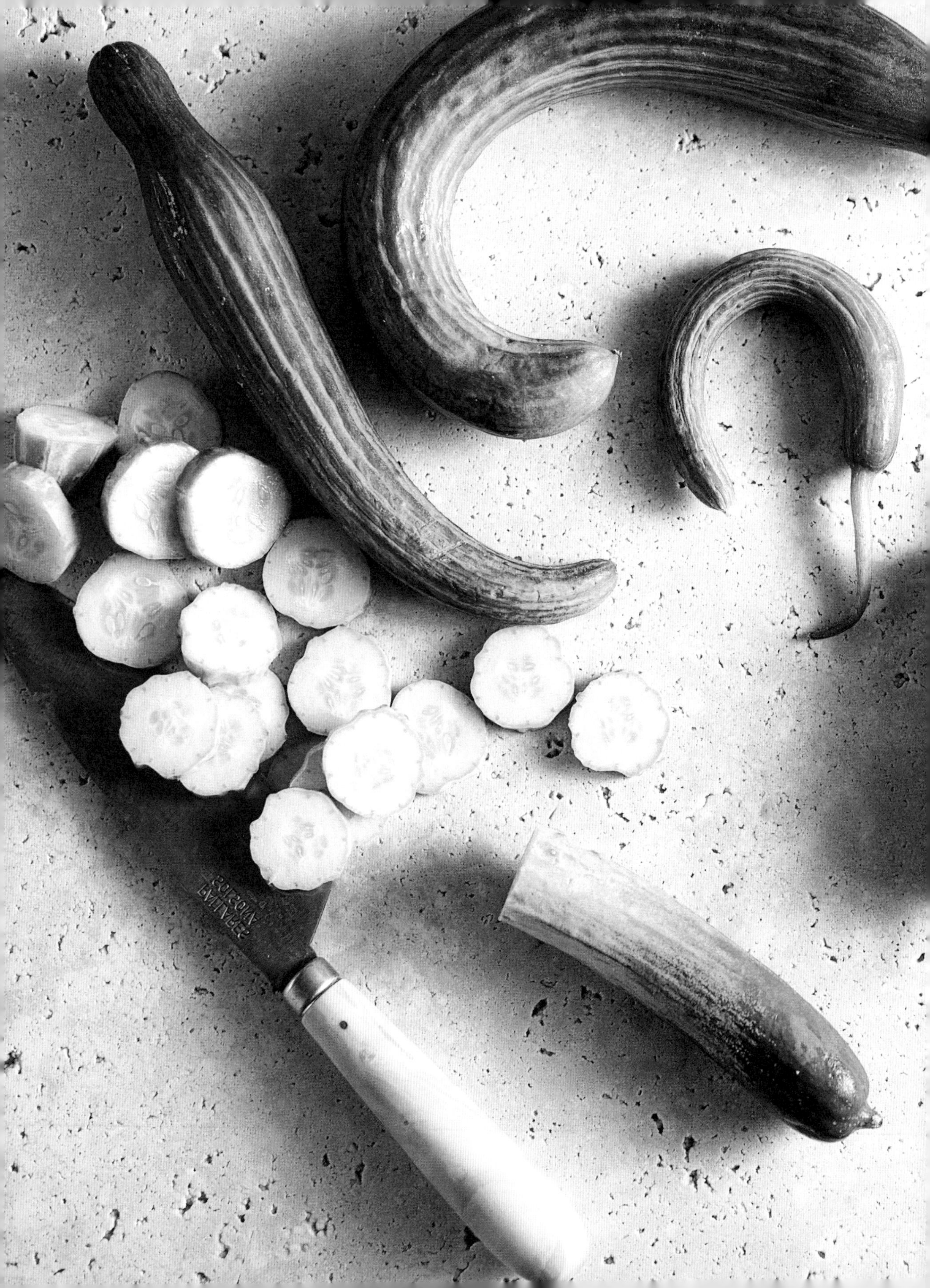

Pickle Party

Condiments are a must-have in my fridge at all times — whip up these easy pickles when produce is abundant to enjoy year-round.

Cook's Note

If there isn't enough liquid to cover the cabbage completely, top it up with some water and a pinch of salt.

Beetroot Sauerkraut

Making sauerkraut at home doesn't have to be a big ordeal. It takes a few minutes of prep and then you can sit back and watch as nature takes its course. This vibrant ruby red condiment is great in sandwiches, breakfast bowls, tacos and salads. It's only slightly fermented so retains crunch and freshness which is just how I like it — full of good bacteria for an energised body and a healthy gut.

Ingredients

3 cups cabbage, finely sliced
1 cup raw beetroot, grated
1 tbsp salt
1 tsp cumin seeds
1 large outer cabbage leaf

Makes *1 jar*
Takes *20 minutes, plus fermentation time*

Gluten-free | Dairy-free | Vegan

Method

Mix cabbage and beetroot together in a large bowl. Sprinkle over salt and massage with your hands for 3–4 minutes, until the cabbage starts to soften. Add cumin seeds, cover the bowl with a tea towel and let it stand for 1–2 hours, to draw more liquid out of the cabbage and beetroot.

Pack the mixture into a sterilised jar, pressing it down with your fist as you go. Pour in any excess juice. Place a large cabbage leaf on top of the mixture, pressing down to make sure all of the sauerkraut is fully submerged in the liquid.

Cover the jar with a clean tea towel, or the lid with a little opening — you want it to be able to breathe. Leave on the counter for 24 hours, occasionally pressing down on the cabbage to compress.

Leave on the counter for 3–4 days, occasionally pressing down on the cabbage. Taste, and when the sauerkraut has reached a sourness that you are happy with, secure the lid and refrigerate until needed.

Tip *Sauerkraut will keep for at least 2 months in the fridge but make sure it's not exposed to air. As long as it's submerged in the sauerkraut juices, it's good to eat. Don't eat sauerkraut that looks mouldy or has been in contact with mouldy scum near the surface.*

Bread & Butter Pickles

This recipe is inspired by another Jess on the JUK team. She brought me in a jar of her homemade bread & butter pickles and I instantly wanted to make my own. I'm not really one for measuring so use this as a rough guide, but it's a great way to use up a glut of zucchini when they're in season. Perfect paired with cheese and bread, or add to our Left Over Roast Beef Sarnie on pg 114 for extra crunch and zing.

Ingredients

10 zucchini, finely sliced
3 large onions, finely sliced
¼ cup salt
3 cups white wine vinegar
2 cups sugar
1 tsp turmeric
1 tsp celery seeds
2 tbsp mustard seeds
2 fresh bay leaves
2 tbsp cornflour

***Makes** 8 cups*
***Takes** 30 minutes, plus overnight soaking*

Gluten-free | Dairy-free | Vegan

Method

Place the zucchini and onions in a bowl. Sprinkle with salt and add just enough cold water to cover. Refrigerate overnight.

Drain the zucchini and onions thoroughly. Place all of the remaining ingredients except for the cornflour into a large saucepan. Bring to the boil and stir to dissolve the sugar.

Mix cornflour with a tablespoon of boiling water until you have a smooth paste. Add to the large pot and boil for two minutes until the liquid thickens slightly.

Add the drained vegetables and bring back to the boil for two more minutes.

Ladle into sterilised jars and seal tightly. Allow jars to cool and store in a cool, dark place for up to 6 months.

Tip You can eat this pickle pretty much straight away! Store in the fridge once opened.

Cook's Note

Add fish sauce instead of miso if you're not fussed about keeping this recipe vegan. And swap soy sauce for tamari to keep this kimchi gluten-free.

Homemade Vegan Kimchi

Traditional Korean kimchi is pungent, tangy and bubbling with living, healthy bacteria. If you're buying kimchi, make sure it's in the refrigerated section of the supermarket — that way you know it's alive — and check for MSG and preservatives. Almost any vegetable can be fermented so kimchi comes in many forms — it's easy to prepare at home and you can make it exactly how you like it!

Ingredients

1 napa or savoy cabbage, outer leaves removed
1 tbsp salt
2 tbsp soy sauce
2 tbsp miso paste
1 tbsp brown sugar
¼ cup pineapple juice
¼ cup warm water
1 thumb-sized knob fresh ginger, peeled and chopped
¼ cup garlic cloves, peeled
1 onion, roughly chopped
½ cup dried chilli flakes (more or less according to your taste)
2 carrots, peeled & grated
1 daikon, peeled & grated
6 spring onions, roughly chopped

Makes *2 large jars*
Takes *20 minutes, plus fermentation time*

Dairy-free | Vegan

Method

Quarter the cabbage length ways, and remove the core. Cut into large squares. Place cabbage in a bowl with the salt and toss to coat well. Place something heavy on top of the cabbage and leave to soften for 1 hour.

Rinse the cabbage under cold water and leave to drain in a colander for 20 minutes.

Meanwhile, make the spice paste. Place the soy sauce, miso, brown sugar, pineapple juice, water, ginger, garlic, onion and chilli flakes into a food processor and blitz into a paste. Taste and adjust as needed. You might want to start with half the quantity of chilli flakes and add more as you go!

Place the drained cabbage in a large bowl and add the carrots, daikon and spring onions, tossing to combine. Add the spice paste to the bowl and coat everything thoroughly with the sauce. You may want to use gloves for this step.

With clean hands, pack the mixture into sterilised jar, pressing it down with your fist as you go. You want as little air between the leaves as possible. Secure the jars with lids and leave in a cool, dark place for 48 hours – 1 week, depending how fermented you want the flavour to be. Occasionally press down on the cabbage to remove air bubbles. Taste, and when the kimchi has reached a sourness that you are happy with, pop it in the refrigerator and use as needed.

Cook's Note

Use caramelised onions as the base of a tart, or alongside a sharp cheddar on your next cheeseboard.

Caramelised Onions

It amazes me how a potent raw onion can transform into a sweet, soft and sticky side dish with just a couple of ingredients and some time. Brown sugar and balsamic help the onions to caramelise in their natural sugars, and this condiment is a delectable accompaniment to cold meats, in burgers or in sandwiches.

Ingredients

2 tbsp olive oil
3 large onions, sliced
2 tbsp brown sugar
2 tbsp balsamic vinegar

Makes *2 cups*
Takes *45 minutes*

Gluten-free | Dairy-free | Vegan

Method

Heat olive oil a heavy saucepan over medium heat. Add the onions and a good pinch of salt and cook the onions, reducing the heat to low, for 15–20 minutes, stirring occasionally.

When the onions are softened and slightly golden, add the sugar and balsamic vinegar. Continue to cook over low heat for another 10–15 minutes, stirring occasionally to prevent the onions from catching, until sticky, dark brown and caramelised.

Use straight away or spoon the caramelised onions into a clean container or jar and store in the fridge.

Tip *Experiment with adding other flavours when you add the sugar and balsamic vinegar — I sometimes add a pinch of chilli flakes and some fresh thyme leaves for that extra little pop.*

A big batch will keep for weeks in the fridge (if they last that long).

单价(元/千克)

Dill Cucumber Pickles

American-style pickles have made a huge comeback in recent years, and it's not hard to see why — crunchy, sweet spears of pickled cucumber that are perfect for cutting through the flavours of rich barbecued meats or gooey grilled cheese sandwiches. Look for small cucumbers — Kirby or Persian are best — as they retain their crunch and firmness better than telegraph cucumbers.

Ingredients

4 cups water
2 cups white wine vinegar
2 tbsp salt
1 tbsp caster sugar
8–10 small cucumbers
4 cloves garlic, smashed
Handful fresh dill, finely diced
1 tsp whole black peppercorns

***Makes** 1 large jar*
***Takes** 15 minutes*

Method

To make the brine add water, vinegar, salt and sugar to a medium-sized saucepan and bring to the boil. Stir to dissolve the sugar and salt. Remove from the heat and cool to room temperature.

Slice cucumbers lengthways into spears and place upright in a clean jar. Add the garlic, dill and peppercorns. Pour the brine over the cucumbers until they are completely submerged. Seal tightly with a lid and store in the fridge for a week before eating.

These refrigerator pickles will last for up to 6 weeks in the fridge.

***Tip** Use this recipe as a template for pickling other vegetables — green beans and carrots also make delicious pickles if you're feeling like branching out into other parts of the garden! You can even reuse the brine and add more fresh cucumbers when your pickles run out.*

Easy Pickled Oranges

My friend who lives in Raglan has an incredible Seville orange tree — juicy and tart and full of sooo much flavour — in the winter when her tree is dripping with fruit and we're sick of making marmalade, we have a jarring session and make masses of these pickled oranges to enjoy in spring and summer.

Ingredients

3 ½ cups caster sugar
1 cup Pedro Ximenex, or sherry*
1 cup white wine vinegar
6 whole black peppercorns
2 cardamom pods
2 whole star anise
8 whole allspice
1 cinnamon quill
1 cup water
8 oranges
1 tsp salt

Makes *3–4 jars*
Takes *1 ½ hours*

Gluten-free | Dairy-free | Vegan

**Pedro Ximenez wine is a sweet dessert wine made from raisins. Like sherry, it is fortified with alcohol after fermenting. You can use a sherry or a vermouth instead.*

Method

Place oranges and salt in a large saucepan and cover with water. Top with a saucer to keep the oranges submerged. Bring to the boil and then reduce heat to low. Cook oranges for 1 hour. Strain, allow to cool slightly, and then cut each orange into thin wedges.

In another large saucepan combine sugar, Pedro Ximinez, vinegar, peppercorns, cardamom, star anise, allspice and cinnamon and water. Bring to the boil over medium heat, stirring until sugar dissolves, and cook for 10 minutes or until reduced slightly.

Add orange wedges to the syrup and cook for 30 more minutes, for the flavour to infuse. Fill steralised jars with oranges and top with syrup. Seal tightly with a lid and invert the jars, allowing them to cool.

Store pickled oranges in a cool, dark place for at least a month before using. Serve with ice cream or natural yoghurt, or finely sliced through a couscous salad. The jars make fantastic Christmas gifts.

Tip *To sterilize jars, wash metal lids and jars, dry and then place on a baking tray in a 120°C oven for 20 minutes. Remove and fill jars while they're still hot.*

Saucy Staples

Minimal effort and huge reward – taking the time to make your own sauces and rubs will lift your home cooking to the next level!

Fennel, Orange & Chilli Salt

This is my favourite combination of citrus and spice — I sprinkle it on eggs, popcorn, roast veges and more — even caramel sauce! If you have a spare salt mill lying around, pop this mix inside so you can easily grind a flavourful pop of salty goodness onto any dish.

Ingredients

2 tsp fennel seeds
1 tsp chilli flakes
Zest from 1 orange, dehydrated or oven dried
1 cup flaky sea salt

***Makes** 1 cup*
***Takes** 10 minutes*

Gluten-free | Dairy-free | Vegan

Method

Place fennel seeds, chilli flakes and orange zest into a mortar & pestle, or a coffee or spice grinder. Pound, or pulse, until well ground. Add the sea salt and mix well to combine, taking care not to pulverize the salt. Taste and increase the amount of flavourings, if required.

Store in an airtight container — the flavours will diminish over time but it will last for up to a year.

Here are some other great flavoured salt combinations to try:

- lemon rosemary salt: ¼ cup salt, ½ tsp dried lemon zest, ½ tsp dried rosemary
- Mexican chilli lime salt: ¼ cup salt, 1 tsp chilli flakes, 1 tsp dried lime zest, ¼ tsp smoked paprika
- lavender salt: ¼ cup salt, 1 tsp dried lavender buds
- vanilla cinnamon salt: ¼ cup salt, ¼ tsp ground cinnamon, seeds from 1 vanilla pod

***Tip** Ingredients such as fresh herbs and citrus zest can be dehydrated in the oven at a low temperature. Spread on a lined baking sheet and place into the oven at 80°C with the door slightly ajar. Check frequently — you want the herbs to be bone dry but not burnt. It may take a few hours for woodier herbs like rosemary and thyme.*

Flavoured Butters

Flavoured butters are great to have on hand – make a batch and keep them in the freezer to serve alongside meat and fish dishes, or toss through warm vegetables.

Café de Paris Butter

Traditionally served with sirloin steak, this is a French bistro favourite. Serve tossed through potatoes, or with fried eggs.

Ingredients: 1 cup parsley leaves, 250g butter, softened, 4 anchovy fillets, 2 tbsp capers, 1 tbsp orange zest, 1 clove garlic, crushed, 2 tbsp tomato ketchup, 1 tbsp Dijon mustard, 1 tbsp Worcestershire sauce, ½ tsp curry powder, ½ tsp smoked paprika, salt & pepper

Method: Place the parsley leaves in a small food processor and pulse until finely chopped. Add the rest of the ingredients and season with salt and freshly ground black pepper. Blitz until well combined. Place Café de Paris butter on a sheet of baking paper and roll into a log, twisting both ends to seal. Refrigerate for 2 hours, or until firm.

Mexican Butter

Smear this over hot corn when it's in season for a taste of Mexico.

Ingredients: 1 cup coriander leaves, 1 cup freshly grated Parmesan, 250g butter, softened, 1 tbsp lime zest, 1 tbsp brown sugar, 1 tbsp lime juice, 1 tbsp smoked paprika, 1 tbsp ground cumin, 1 tsp dried chilli flakes, salt & pepper

Method: Place the coriander leaves in a small food processor and pulse until finely chopped. Add the rest of the ingredients and season with salt and freshly ground black pepper. Blitz until well combined. Place Mexican butter on a sheet of baking paper and roll into a log, twisting both ends to seal. Refrigerate for 2 hours, or until firm.

Mint Butter

This is delicious on baby potatoes or tossed through peas.

Ingredients: 4 cups mint leaves, 1 tbsp lemon zest, 1 tbsp brown sugar, 1 tbsp white wine vinegar, 250g butter, softened, salt & pepper

Method: Place the mint leaves in a small food processor and pulse until finely chopped. Add the lemon zest, sugar, vinegar, butter and season with salt & freshly ground black pepper. Blitz until well combined. Place mint butter on a sheet of baking paper and roll into a log, twisting both ends to seal. Refrigerate for 2 hours, or until firm.

Nori & Sesame Butter

Seaweed butter brings a taste of umami to any side dish, or simply slather over fresh bread.

Ingredients: 2 sheets nori (dried seaweed), 2 tsp black sesame seeds, 1 tbsp lemon zest, 1 clove garlic, crushed, 1 tsp chilli flakes, 250g butter, softened, salt & pepper

Method: Roughly tear the nori and place in a small food processor and pulse until finely chopped. Add the sesame seeds, lemon zest, garlic, chilli flakes, butter and season with salt & freshly ground black pepper. Blitz until well combined. Place nori butter on a sheet of baking paper and roll into a log, twisting both ends to seal. Refrigerate for 2 hours, or until firm.

Cinnamon Honey Butter

Take your pancakes up a notch with this whipped butter. Also delicious melted over roast kumara or pumpkin!

Ingredients: 250g butter, softened, 1 cup icing sugar, 3 tbsp honey, 1 tsp vanilla extract, 1 tbsp ground cinnamon, 1 tsp salt

Method: Place all of the ingredients into the bowl of a stand mixer fitted with a paddle attachment. Beat until well combined and fluffy. Place cinnamon honey butter on a sheet of baking paper and roll into a log, twisting both ends to seal. Refrigerate for 2 hours, or until firm. Serve at room temperature.

Grated Tomato Dressing

Make this dressing in the middle of summer when tomatoes are ripe and abundant. Seconds or bruised tomatoes work really well here, as a little softness doesn't matter. If you want to get really fancy, cut an X in the bottom of each tomato, drop them in boiling water for 20 seconds and peel the skin off before grating.

Ingredients

4 large, ripe tomatoes, halved
1 clove garlic, finely diced
¼ cup red wine vinegar
1 tbsp honey
¼ cup extra virgin olive oil

***Makes** 1 cup*
***Takes** 10 minutes*

Gluten-free | Dairy-free | Vegan

Method

Place an upright grater in a wide bowl and grate tomatoes on the largest holes until all that's left is the flattened skin — discard. Season tomatoes generously with salt and pepper.

Add the garlic, vinegar and honey to the bowl and whisk to combine. While continuously whisking, slowly pour in the olive oil. Taste and season again if necessary.

You can store this dressing in the fridge for up to three days.

Tip *Turn this dressing into the freshest of pasta sauces by bringing it to a gentle simmer in a saucepan and reducing for 5–10 minutes. Add fresh herbs and a dab of butter when you take it off the heat. Perfect for lazy summer suppers!*

Pesto — Three Ways

I still buy store-bought pesto when I'm in a rush, but making your own is so easy once you know how, and there are so many rifts on the recipe that you'll pretty much always have the basics on hand to whip up a batch. Here is my basic basil pesto recipe, along with three variations to suit your dietary requirements or simply what you have in your pantry or fridge.

Ingredients

2 cups fresh basil leaves
2 cloves garlic, crushed
½ cup grated Parmesan
½ cup toasted pine nuts
1 tsp lemon juice
½ cup olive oil

Makes 1 cup
Takes 10 minutes

Gluten-free

Method

Pound together the basil, garlic, Parmesan and pine nuts in a mortar & pestle. Once you have a smooth paste, add the lemon juice and drizzle in the oil, mixing to combine. Season with salt and freshly ground black pepper.

Alternatively, place all of the ingredients in a food processor and blitz until smooth. Pulse if you prefer a more textured consistency.

Change the greens

Kale, rocket, cavalo nero, parsley, coriander, chervil, sorrel, watercress, mint, peas, broccoli or move away from greens completely and use sundried tomatoes, roasted capsicum or even carrot.

Change the nuts

Walnuts, almonds, pistachios, cashews, macadamia nuts all make for a delicious pesto. If you have a nut allergy (or for a more cost-effective option), use sunflower, sesame or pumpkin seeds.

Change the cheese

Hard cheeses work well — try Gruyère for a nutty taste, manchego, aged cheddar, pecorino or Grana Padano.
If you want your pesto to be vegan, leave out the cheese completely. You can substitute ½ cup of nutritional yeast to give your pesto that 'cheesy' flavour.

Orange, Caper & Basil Salsa

Sometimes we need more than a sauce but less than a salad... and that's when my friend the salsa steps in. This citrus number is fantastic with barbecued fish, salmon, eggplant steaks or pulled pork tacos and it's so adaptable. If you don't have preserved lemon, add a decent hit of lemon zest instead.

Ingredients

2 oranges, segmented and finely diced
½ preserved lemon, skin only, finely diced
½ small red onion, finely diced
2 tbsp capers, drained and rinsed
Handful fresh basil leaves, half finely chiffonaded and half reserved for serving
1 tbsp olive oil
½ tsp chilli flakes
½ tsp fennel seeds

***Makes** 4 serves*
***Takes** 10 minutes, plus 30 minutes marinating time*

Gluten-free | Dairy-free | Vegan

Method

Gently combine of the ingredients in a bowl and place in the fridge for 30 minutes to marinate. Season with salt and freshly ground black pepper to taste. Serve with extra basil leaves.

***Tip** To add a spicy Mexican twist, include a tablespoon of jalapeño juice and a couple of finely diced jalapeño peppers to your salsa while it marinates, and swap out the basil for coriander.*

Labneh

One of the pillars of Middle Eastern cuisine, labneh is a soft cheese made from strained yoghurt, and it's so easy to make at home. You can enjoy it with sweet or savoury accompaniments: serve it up as a dip with seasonal vegetables, a good glug of olive oil and some dukkah sprinkled on top. Or it's just as delicious topped with grilled peaches, pistachios and a drizzle of honey for a simple dessert.

Ingredients

2 cups plain Greek yoghurt
½ tsp salt
1 tsp lemon juice

***Makes** 1 cup*
***Takes** 5 minutes, plus 12–24 hours straining time*

Method

Line a sieve with a few layers of cheesecloth or muslin and set it above a large pot or bowl. If you don't have cheesecloth, a clean Chux cloth or similar will work well here, too. Set 2–3 layers at different angles to make sure you can cover the whole ball of yoghurt without it spilling over the edges.

In a bowl, mix together the yoghurt, salt and lemon juice. Spoon it into the cloth-lined sieve and pull the layers of cloth up so that the yoghurt hangs in a ball. Discard the sieve and tie the cloth around a wooden spoon or something long enough to suspend it over the pot without the ball touching the bottom. The pot will collect the whey as it's strained off the yoghurt.

Place the pot and clothed yoghurt ball in the fridge for 12–24 hours, to continue straining. The longer you leave it for, the thicker the labneh.

Remove the strained yoghurt from the fridge and unfold the cloth to reveal a labneh ball. Serve straight away, or store in an airtight container in the fridge for up to two weeks.

Tip *Don't throw the whey away! There's a lot of goodness in there. Add this bi-product to smoothies for a protein hit, make my green whey salad dressing, see page 53, use it in risotto for extra flavour and nutrients, feed it to your plants (tomatoes love the extra calcium hit) or your pets! Apparently it's super good for them, too.*

Cook's Note

Use a good quality yoghurt when you make this, as you'll get a better yield (and resulting taste).

Beetroot Yoghurt Dip with Pistachios

Quick and easy, no one will be able to resist the vibrant colour of this beetroot-spiked dip at your next gathering! You can cook your own beetroot from scratch but in this instance I use canned beets for their time-saving ease. Serve by itself with crackers for a casual snack or as part of a inspired platter for a healthy and tasty meal.

Ingredients

1 450g can of baby beetroot, drained
3–4 garlic cloves
1 ½ cups natural yoghurt
¼ cup lemon juice
2 tbsp olive oil
½ tsp ground cumin
½ tsp ground coriander
½ tsp ground cinnamon
½ tsp smoked paprika
2 tbsp toasted pistachios

Makes *6 serves as a starter*
Takes *10 minutes*

Method

Place the beetroot and garlic in a food processor and blend to form a chunky paste. Add ½ cup of yoghurt, lemon juice, olive oil, cumin, coriander, cinnamon and paprika. Blend to form a smooth puree. Taste and season with salt and freshly ground black pepper.

Place the remaining cup of yoghurt in a serving bowl. Pour the beetroot puree into the middle and use a spoon to softly marble it through the yoghurt. Top with pistachio nuts to serve.

Tip *The beetroot puree can also be used as a base for beetroot hummus. Omit the yoghurt and instead add a can of drained chickpeas and 2 tablespoons of tahini. Drizzle in some extra olive oil while the food processor is running until you get a smooth, creamy (bright pink!) hummus.*

Green Whey Salad Dressing

I know this sounds a bit weird, but whey is so full of nutrients and a great way to use it up is in a salad dressing! If you've made my labneh, see page 44, and have a jar of whey hanging out in your fridge, give this a go. It's lighter and more subtle than most of my dressings but makes for the perfect no waste palate refresher when paired with a fresh and simple salad.

Ingredients

1 garlic clove, finely diced
Handful fresh herbs — parsley, dill or coriander are my favourites
1 tbsp Dijon mustard
¼ cup whey
2 tbsp white wine vinegar
¼ cup olive oil

Makes *1 cup*
Takes *5 minutes*

Method

Place the garlic and parsley in a food processor and pulse until a paste is formed. Add the remaining ingredients and blend into a smooth dressing. Taste and season with salt and freshly ground black pepper.

Store in an airtight jar in the fridge for up to 5 days.

Tip *Fun fact: whey helps stimulate the kidneys to release toxins and it's also known to help reduce fluid retention!*

Homemade Vanilla Extract

Once you've made this yourself, you'll never buy the imitation vanilla from the supermarket again. It's so much more cost efficient than the store-brought stuff, plus it tastes a hundred times better. You can use the extract after 6 weeks, but it'll develop even better flavour after 6 months or longer.

Ingredients

9 whole vanilla beans
3 cups vodka

Makes *3 cups*
Takes *5 minutes, plus 6 weeks extraction time*

Gluten-free | Dairy-free | Vegan

Method

Slice each pod lengthways and place in a clean bottle or jar. Pour in the vodka so the vanilla beans are completely submerged. Fasten the lid and give it a good shake.

Store in a cool, dark place and shake once or twice a week, when you remember.

Tip *If you don't have vodka handy you can also use Bourbon, rum or brandy — any brand or quality is fine. It's the quality of the vanilla beans, not the alcohol, that'll give you the best flavour!*

Cook's Note

Red or yellow capsicums work best for this harissa as they are sweeter, plus give a great orange colour. For an extra-smooth, creamy sauce, use a high-powered blender instead of a food processor.

Harissa Dressing

It's hard not to love this smoky, spicy roasted pepper sauce. You can experiment with different fresh or dried chillies, or add different spices to suit your taste — rose, caraway and even mint are all welcome additions. Try adding a dollop of harissa to the top of some store-bought hummus to pimp up to your next cheese platter. Or serve this with roasted chicken and a crunchy cos salad.

Ingredients

4 capsicum
1 onion, peeled and roughly chopped
½ cup olive oil
1 tsp coriander seeds
1 tsp cumin seeds
1 tsp fennel seeds
4 tbsp olive oil
3 garlic cloves
1–2 tsp chilli flakes (to taste)
1 lemon, zested and juiced

Makes *2 cups*
Takes *40 minutes*

Gluten-free | Dairy-free | Vegan

Method

Preheat oven to 200°C. Place the capsicums and onion on a lined baking tray and drizzle with a tablespoon of the olive oil. Toast until charred, turning once, around 20–25 minutes. Transfer the capsicums to a bowl and cover with glad wrap for 5 minutes. Once cool enough to handle, peel off the charred skins and discard the stem and the seeds. Return the capsicum flesh to the tray with the onions.

Place a small frying pan over medium heat and toast off the coriander, cumin and fennel seeds for 1–2 minutes, until fragrant and slightly browned. Transfer into a food processor and pulse until finely ground.

Add the capsicum and onions to the food processor, plus all of the remaining ingredients, and blitz until smooth. Add more olive oil or lemon juice if necessary. Taste and season with salt and freshly ground black pepper.

Store in an airtight container in the fridge for up to three weeks.

Tahini Jar Dressing

I absolutely HATE throwing away jars that still contain the dregs of expensive products and my favourite way to repurpose them is to turn them into salad dressing jars! This turmeric-spiked tahini dressing is creamy and delicious, perfect for drizzling over roasted vegetables or in a fresh, summery salad like this one.

Ingredients

3 tbsp tahini paste, or the remnants in the bottom of the jar to roughly the same quantity
3 tbsp boiling water
3 tbsp lemon juice
2 tbsp olive oil
½ tsp ground turmeric
½ tsp cayenne pepper

Makes *½ cup*
Takes *10 minutes*

Gluten-free | Dairy-free | Vegan

Method

Add the tahini paste and boiling water to a jar, secure the lid tightly and shake until the water and tahini are smooth and combined. Add the remaining ingredients, secure the lid and shake again until well combined. If you'd prefer a runnier dressing, add more water. Season to taste with salt and freshly ground black pepper.

Tip *Scale this recipe up and make extra — it'll keep well in the fridge for up to 10 days.*

I always keep the liquids that come in my gherkin, jalapeño and pickle jars as well — these are great for adding to salad dressings and sauces that benefit from an extra flavour kick — never throw them away!!

Cook's Note

If your caramel has solidified in the fridge, sit it in a bowl of hot water for a few minutes, or remove the lid and gently heat in short bursts in the microwave before using.

Bacon Caramel

Take your vanilla ice-cream to the next stratosphere with this smoky bacon-infused caramel sauce – the ultimate play on salty sweet. Sometimes I save the bacon dripping across several breakfasts to get enough to make an extra-large batch. I always use salted butter as it adds a salty layer to this caramel but if you think it needs an extra pop to balance the sweetness, add another pinch of salt.

Ingredients

4 slices streaky bacon
½ cup cream
½ cup water
1 cup sugar
5 tbsp butter

***Makes** 2 cups*
***Takes** 30 minutes*

Gluten-free

Method

In a heavy bottomed frying pan or skillet over high heat, fry the bacon until extra crispy. Remove the pan from the heat and drain the bacon on paper towels to one side. Add the cream to the pan and let it stand to infuse.

Place the water and sugar in a small saucepan over medium heat. Boil, without stirring, until it turns a light golden brown, swirling the pan every once in a while to ensure the colour is even.

Add the bacon-infused cream and butter to the caramel mixture and stir rapidly until the butter is melted. The caramel will bubble up furiously so be careful not to burn yourself with sugar mixture or steam. Keep stirring until the caramel is smooth and drizzle-thickness — bear in mind it'll keep thickening as it cools.

Dice the cooked bacon and either add it to your caramel for extra bacon-ness or use as a topping over ice cream.

You can use the bacon caramel straight away or spoon into a clean container or jar and store in the fridge for up to a week.

Breakfast Club

I don't usually make much time for breakfast during the week, but come the weekend it's my favourite meal of the day — treat yourself like a champion with these easy and inspiring eats.

juk.

Negroni Marmalade

If you're in need of an early morning tipple, reach no further than this orange & grapefruit Campari-spiked spread to slosh over your toast. Jokes aside, the addition of Campari adds a delicious bitter-sweetness and while the alcohol is cooked off during the process, it's a super fun edible gift and one of my favourite weekend breakfast treats! I love it on a cheese platter with a ripe brie and a funky blue, too.

Ingredients

4 oranges
2 grapefruit
1 ½ cups Campari
3 cups white sugar
1 cinnamon stick
2 star anise
1 vanilla pod, sliced in half and seeds scraped out

Makes *8 cups*
Takes *1 hour, plus overnight*

Dairy-free | Gluten-free | Vegan

Method

Remove the ends from the oranges and grapefruit, plus any visible seeds or excess pith. Quarter and slice into thin slices.

Place in a large bowl along with any excess juice and fill with cold water until the citrus is just covered. Cover the bowl and place in the fridge overnight.

Place the citrus and water in a large saucepan and add the sugar, Campari, cinnamon, star anise, vanilla seeds and vanilla pod, stirring well to dissolve the sugar. Bring to a gentle simmer and cook, stirring regularly, until the mixture is reduced by half. Remove cinnamon stick, star anise and vanilla pod.

Pour marmalade into clean, sterilised jars and allow to cool completely before lidding and storing.

Tip *Use a couple of tablespoons of this marmalade to make the best ever Christmas ham glaze,* *see page 243.*

One Skillet Breakfast Frittata

The beauty of this breakfast frittata is that everything is done in one pan. The fewer the dishes, the happier I am! This is a one-person recipe but you can scale it up depending on how many people you want to feed; either make individual serves in individual skillets or make a larger frittata in one big skillet — just cook a bit longer until the middle of the frittata feels set and leave it to cool in the pan for easier slicing.

Ingredients

1 tbsp olive oil
½ onion, sliced
2 garlic cloves, smashed
2 rashers streaky bacon, roughly chopped
½ tsp chilli flakes
½ tsp mixed herbs
2 eggs, whisked
Handful spinach leaves
¼ cup grated Parmesan cheese
1 small vine tomato, halved

Makes *1 x 12cm frittata*
Takes *25 minutes*

Gluten-free

Method

Preheat oven to 180°C. Heat a 12cm cast iron skillet over medium-high heat and add olive oil and onions. Saute for 1–2 minutes, until onions are starting to sweat. Add garlic and cook for another minute.

Scrape onion mixture to one side of the pan and add the bacon. Cook for 1–2 minutes, until lightly browned. Add chilli flakes and mixed herbs, plus a pinch of salt and some freshly ground black pepper, and stir to combine.

Remove the skillet from the heat and add the egg mixture, swirling the pan to distribute evenly. Add spinach leaves, sprinkle with cheese and place the tomatoes on top, cut-side up. Place skillet in the oven and bake for 10–15 minutes, until the middle of the frittata is set.

Allow to cool slightly in the pan before turning out onto a plate to serve.

Tip *Use whatever ingredients you have on hand to make your favourite frittata! I like to add: chorizo, fresh herbs if I have them, a nutty cheese like a Gruyère, a spoonful of tomato relish or even leftover smoked salmon!*

juk.

Gin & Sumac-Cured Salmon

It's a twist on the classic gravlax, but it's one of my new faves. Curing salmon is a great way to make salmon go a long way because, let's face it, salmon is expensive. It's salty and intense so you don't need a lot. Always choose homegrown NZ salmon over Atlantic salmon and the fresher the better.

Ingredients

1 large side of salmon
6 tbsp coarse sea salt
2 tbsp castor sugar
2 tbsp sumac
1 tbsp cumin seeds
6 tbsp gin
Small handful fresh dill, finely chopped
Extra fresh dill, for serving

***Makes** 12 serves*
***Takes** 20 minutes plus 36–48 hours marinating time*

Gluten-free | Dairy-free

Method

Rinse the salmon and pat dry with paper towels. Check for any bones, and remove with kitchen tweezers if necessary.

In a small bowl mix the salt, sugar, sumac, cumin seeds, gin and dill.

Overlap two pieces of plastic wrap on a shallow-lipped baking tray, allowing some to hang over the sides. Place the salmon in the centre of the plastic wrap and cover in the gin mixture. Bring the edges of the plastic wrap up and over the salmon to seal. Place another baking tray on top of the salmon and weigh it down with a couple of heavy tins or chopping boards. Refrigerate for up to two days, turning occasionally.

Thinly slice the salmon, garnish with fresh dill and serve on a large platter with fresh bread and sour cream or nautral yoghurt.

Tip *For perfectly thin gravlax slices, try running your knife blade under warm water before cutting each slice.*

Brunch Pizza — Three Ways

Pizza for breakfast is a great way to feed a hungry crowd, plus it's hard to beat an eggy pizza. Here are three of my favourite toppings. I use store-bought pizza bases here, but you can totally make your own. Tortilla wraps and naan breads also make excellent throw-together pizza bases if you're in a hurry and already have these items in the fridge or freezer.

Caramelised onion, chorizo & mushroom pizza

Lightly pan-fry assorted mushrooms with 2 tbsp olive oil. Season with salt and freshly ground black pepper. Spread the pizza base with store-bought or homemade caramelised onions, see page 21, top with mushroom mixture and some shredded rosemary leaves. Split a fresh chorizo sausage in half and dot the chorizo meat across the top of the mushroom. Crack an egg into the centre and grill for 4–5 minutes, until pizza base is crispy and golden. Drizzle with extra virgin olive oil to serve.

Spinach, smoked salmon & avocado pizza

Thinly spread some cream cheese onto a pizza base and top with baby spinach leaves and avocado slices. Season with salt and freshly cracked pepper. Crack an egg into the centre and grill for 4–5 minutes, until pizza base is crispy and golden. Ribbon cold smoked salmon across the pizza and drizzle with extra virgin olive oil to serve.

Huevos rancheros breakfast pizza

In a small saucepan, sauté ½ a sliced onion with 1 tbsp olive oil. Add 2 tbsp tomato paste, 1 cup of diced tomatoes and 1 cup of drained black beans. Cook for a few minutes until the mixture has thickened slightly. Season with salt and freshly ground black pepper. Spread black bean mixture onto a pizza base. Top with sliced jalapeños, diced tomatoes, crumbled feta and crack an egg into the centre. Grill for 4–5 minutes, until pizza base is crispy and golden. Top with fresh coriander leaves, sliced spring onions and a squeeze of fresh lime juice to serve.

juk.

Breakfast Bologonese Bowl

There's mince on toast, there's poached eggs on toast, and then there's the holy marriage of both: introducing the breakfast Bolognese bowl. In my humble opinion this is the ultimate leftover dish, for two reasons — (1) tomato-based ragus and sauces always taste better the next day, and (2) almost anything is better when it's topped with a perfectly poached egg. You're welcome.

Ingredients

2 tbsp white vinegar
2 tbsp salt
4 eggs
2 cups leftover best Bolognese, *see page 160*
4 cups leftover cooked spaghetti
50g shaved Parmesan
Fresh parsley, to serve

Makes *4 serves*
Takes *15 minutes*

Method

Bring a large pot of water to the boil and add vinegar and salt. With the water at a medium simmer, crack each egg into the water. Cook for 2–3 minutes — check whether they're done by removing an egg from the pot with a slotted spoon and pushing gently on the yolk; if it feels too soft, put it back in and give it another 30 seconds. When the eggs are ready, remove from the water with a slotted spoon and place them on a paper towel.

In a small pan over medium heat, gently reheat the Bolognese. Add a splash of water if it needs a little loosening.

Boil the jug. Place leftover spaghetti in a large bowl and pour over boiling water until it's just covered. Sit for a couple of minutes to warm through, before draining well.

To serve, divide the spaghetti between four bowls. Top with a spoonful of Bolognese and a poached egg. Scatter with Parmesan and parsley just before serving.

Tip *I sometimes save time by reusing the water from my eggs to heat the spaghetti through; just strain through a colander in case there are any stringy bits of egg left in the water.*

Roasted Plums with Thyme & Labneh

This summery dish makes for a lazy breakfast or simple dessert. All of the work can be done in advance! The recipe works wonderfully with any stone fruit — try it out on nectarines, peaches or apricots when you have them on hand. You can also experiment with other woody herbs, like rosemary or sage.

Ingredients

4 slightly under-ripe plums, halved and pitted
1 tbsp brown sugar
4 sprigs thyme, plus small handful of extra thyme leaves for serving
1 knob butter, cut into 8 small pieces
1 cup labneh, see page 44

Makes *4 serves*
Takes *30 minutes*

Method

Preheat oven to 200°C. Halve and de-stone the plums. Place the plum halves, cut side up, in a baking dish. A muffin tray works well here, too. Sprinkle the brown sugar and thyme evenly across the plums. Place a small piece of butter into the centre of each plum.

Roast until the sugar has melted and the skins are just beginning to pucker, 15–20 minutes. Let the plums cool in the baking dish before removing.

To serve, divide the labneh evenly between four plates. Add two plum halves to each plate and spoon over some of the crimson juices from the bottom of the dish. Garnish with extra thyme leaves.

Tip *Using slightly under-ripe plums makes them easier to cut in half and remove the stones. The temperature of the oven and the sugar will help them get to the perfect consistency when they're roasted.*

Blackberry, Sage & Goats' Cheese Jaffle

Equal parts nostalgic and gourmet, we like to get creative with our toasted sandwich fillings at JUK and this is currently one of my faves. With sweetness and herbaciousness (and, of course — cheese!) it's perfectly balanced and a far cry from the marmite & cheese jaffles of my youth (not that there's anything wrong with a mousetrap every once in a while!)

Ingredients

4 slices white toast bread
2 tbsp butter, softened
4 tbsp blackberry jam
50g goats' cheese, crumbled
8 fresh sage leaves

***Makes** 2 serves*
***Takes** 10 minutes*

Method

Preheat a jaffle machine.

Butter 4 slices of bread. Press two sage leaves into the butter of each slide. Flip two slices over so the buttered side is facing down. Spread these two slices with blackberry jam and divide the goats' cheese evenly on top of the jam.

Place the two un-jammed slices on top, butter-side facing up.

Place sandwiches in the jaffle machine and toast for 4–5 minutes, until golden.

***Tip** If you're not a fan of goats' cheese, use ricotta or cream cheese instead. And you can sub blackberry jam for your favourite berry condiment — marmalade works well here, too!*

Olive Oil & Sea Salt Muesli

Once you start making your own muesli, you'll never go back to the store-bought stuff again. This version is the perfect balance of salty and sweet. Pair with your choice of yoghurt, milk and poached fruit for the ultimate breakfast bowl. You can swap out the nuts and raisins for other combinations to find your favourite mix.

Ingredients

3 cups giant rolled oats
1 cup sunflower seeds
1 cup pumpkin seeds
1 cup whole almonds
1 cup whole hazelnuts
¼ cup sesame seeds
½ cup raisins
½ cup olive oil
½ cup honey
2 tsp flaky sea salt
½ cup coconut flakes

Makes *8 cups*
Takes *40 minutes*

Dairy-free

Method

Preheat oven to 180°C. In a large bowl, stir together all of the ingredients except for the coconut flakes, making sure that everything is coated evenly.

Spread out of a lined baking sheet and bake for 30 minutes. Give everything a stir, add the coconut flakes and bake for another 8–10 minutes until golden brown. Remove from the oven and season with extra flaky sea salt, to taste. Allow to cool completely before storing in an airtight container.

Tip *Look for gluten-free rolled oats to make this muesli gluten-free.*

Snack Attack

In lieu of a full meal, an easy and healthy snack is sometimes all we need to keep hunger at bay — these are some of my current favourites.

Salt & Vinegar Edamame

Edamame beans are commonly found in almost all supermarkets nowadays, and it's so easy to have a packet or two of these in the freezer for unexpected snack cravings. I like to have shelled edamame on hand to add to salads and poke bowls, but these unshelled edamame beans make for great party fare. The pods get slightly charred at they cook, adding a next-level smoky flavour to the beans.

Ingredients

450g frozen edamame beans, unshelled
½ cup white vinegar
3 tbsp olive oil
2 tsp flaky sea salt
1 tsp dried chilli flakes

Makes *4–6 servings*
Takes *20 minutes*

Gluten-free | Dairy-free | Vegan

Method

Preheat oven to 180°C. Pour edamame beans into a colander and run under cold water for 10–15 seconds to remove the ice crystals. Drain thoroughly and place in a medium bowl. Pour over vinegar and sit for 5–10 minutes, stirring several times to coat.

Drain the edamame thoroughly and return to the bowl. Add oil and salt, tossing well to coat. Season with freshly ground black pepper.

Spread edamame in a single layer on a large lined baking tray and roast for 20 minutes, stirring once, until shells are starting to brown and serve immediately.

Tip *You can use this recipe with shelled edamame beans, too. Halve the quantities of vinegar and salt and bake for twice as long until they're extra crispy and puffy. Best eaten straight away, so get snacking!*

Cavalo Crisps

Cavalo nero or Tuscan kale is my new favourite 'kale'. It's softer and leafier than its frilly cousin, and is really delicious sliced raw through salads or braised through stews and soups. These nutrient-dense 'crisps' are baked not fried and have a moreish crunch to them. Serve alongside dips, on top of pastas or salads, or simply just by themselves as a healthy snack!

Ingredients

500g cavalo nero
2 tbsp olive oil
1 tsp ground cumin
1 tsp dried chilli flakes
½ tsp smoked paprika
½ tsp turmeric
½ tsp flaky sea salt
lime wedges, to serve

Makes *4 serves*
Takes *20 minutes*

Gluten-free | Dairy-free | Vegan

Method

Preheat oven to 180°C.

Wash the cavalo nero and dry thoroughly. Remove any stalky ends.

Combine the olive oil, cumin, chilli, paprika, turmeric and salt in a large bowl. Add the cavalo nero and toss to coat as evenly as you can. Spread the leaves in a single layer over 1–2 baking trays.

Bake for 12–15 minutes, checking regularly. The cooking time will depend largely on your oven, and you don't want to burn them! Once the leaves are starting to brown slightly and are crisp at the edges, remove from the oven and leave to cool for 5 minutes on the tray. This will help them to crisp up even more.

Serve with some lime wedges for squeezing over.

Tip *It's really important that the leaves are thoroughly dry before you toss them in the oil and spices, otherwise they'll steam while baking. And no one likes a soggy chip!*

PALLARES
SOLSONA

One-Hour Focaccia

This is such an easy bread recipe, and it turns out perfectly every time. You can bake the focaccia plain with salt or add ingredients into the bread before baking for a glorious seasonal twist. Here I've used spring onions and asparagus for a spring brunch recipe, and also topped a salted focaccia with a fresh cherry, basil & goats' cheese salad for my festive twist on a 'caprese'. What will your favourite be?

Ingredients

Focaccia bread

¾ cup warm water
½ tsp sugar
1 ½ tsp instant yeast
6 tbsp good quality olive oil
1 ¾ cups high quality flour
1 tsp salt
1 tbsp flaky salt, for topping

Spring toppings

1 handful asparagus, trimmed
1 handful spring onions, trimmed
½ cup crème fraiche

Summer toppings

1 cup fresh cherries, pitted
1 handful basil leaves, purple & green if you can find them
100g fresh goats' cheese, crumbled
1 tbsp olive oil
½ lemon, zested & juiced

Makes *4 serves*
Takes *60 minutes*

Method

Preheat oven to 100°C.

Place the warm water, sugar and yeast in a small bowl and stir gently. Leave to stand for 5 minutes, until foamy.

In a large bowl, mix together 1 cup of flour and the salt. Make a small well in the centre and pour in the yeast mixture. Mix together gently until combined. Add 2 tablespoons of olive oil and mix until combined. Gradually at the remaining flour and turn out onto a floured surface, kneading gently until you have a smooth ball of dough.

Grease a skillet or a shallow pan with 2 tablespoons of olive oil and place the dough in the middle, gently pressing it into a flat disk to take on the shape of the pan. Drizzle with 2 more tablespoons of olive oil. Cover pan with a clean tea towel.

Place pan in the oven and turn the oven off. Let the bread rise for 20 minutes. Remove the pan from the oven and remove the tea towel.

Preheat oven to 200°C.

Gently press down on the bread with your fingers, to create little dimples all over.

To make spring focaccia: *Trim the asparagus and spring onions to size and place lengthways across the focaccia. Sprinkle with sea salt and drizzle with extra olive oil. Bake for 20 minutes, or until golden brown. Allow to cool slightly on a rack before dotting with crème fraiche before serving.*

To make summer focaccia: *Sprinkle with sea salt. Bake for 20 minutes, or until golden brown. In a small bowl, toss together the salad ingredients, seasoning with salt and freshly ground black pepper, and scatter on top of the focaccia before serving.*

Beetroot Pickled Eggs

These fuschia pickled eggs will add a pop of colour to your next Ploughmans platter or picnic spread! Keep a jar in your fridge — the longer you keep the eggs in the pickling liquid, the deeper the beautiful pink will penetrate. Play around with different spices in your pickling brine, too.

Ingredients

10 hard-boiled eggs, peeled
1 beetroot, peeled and roughly chopped into cubes
2 cups water
1 cup cider vinegar
½ cup sugar
1 tsp salt
2 whole star anise
3 cardamom pods
1 whole cinnamon quill
8 black peppercorns

***Makes** 10 pickled eggs*
***Takes** 30 minutes*

Gluten-free | Dairy-free

Method

Bring water, vinegar, sugar and salt up to a boil in a large saucepan. Add the chopped beetroot and simmer for 25–30 minutes, until the beetroot is tender.

Let the beetroot cool and strain the juices into a resealable glass jar. Add the eggs, star anise, cardamom, cinnamon and peppercorns. Seal and refrigerate for at least 4 hours before serving. They'll last for up to 3 weeks in the fridge.

***Tip** Make an instant beetroot brine by straining the juice from a can of beetroot and mixing it directly with vinegar, sugar and salt.*

Mediterranean Baked Feta

Grilled cheese is a big thing in Europe and we really don't embrace it enough here in the southern hemisphere! I'm not talking about melty mozzarella or cheddar, I'm talking about saganaki or haloumi or giant slabs of oven-roasted feta — if you've had it you know what I'm talking about. This rustic version encaptures all of the heady flavours of a European summer.

Ingredients

200g feta cheese
½ cup cherry tomatoes
½ cup Kalamata olives
2 sprigs fresh thyme
2 cloves garlic, smashed
½ lemon, thinly sliced
1 tsp dried chilli flakes
1 tsp fennel seeds
2 tbsp olive oil

Makes *4 serves*
Takes *20 minutes*

Method

Preheat oven to 200°C.

Place feta in a small ovenproof dish. Add the tomatoes, olives, thyme, garlic and lemon around the sides. Sprinkle the chilli and fennel seeds on top of the feta and drizzle all over with olive oil. Season with salt and freshly ground black pepper.

Bake for 15–20 minutes until the tomatoes are blistered and the feta is softened.

Tip *Serve with crackers, toast or vegetable crudités.*

Marinated Labneh Balls

This is a great way to preserve your labneh to use at a later date, plus it's a beautiful edible gift if you're so inclined! They're gorgeous served in a bowl as part of a mezze platter, or spread on crackers. Try different flavour combinations and find your favourite!

Ingredients

5 tsp dried chilli flakes
5 tsp chopped parsley
5 tsp lemon zest
2 cups labneh, see page 44
3 cups extra virgin olive oil

***Makes** 6–8 as a snack*
***Takes** 15 minutes*

Gluten-free

Method

Mix the chilli, parsley and lemon zest together and spread on a shallow plate.

Pinch off a walnut-sized piece of labneh and roll into a ball with your hands. Roll the ball in the herb mixture until well coated and place in a clean jar. Repeat until the jar is full. Pour in the olive oil until all of the labneh balls are completely submerged, and fasten the lid.

Store in a cool, dark place for up to two months. Once opened, use within two weeks.

You can keep the labneh balls in the fridge, but just bear in mind that the oil will solidify. No worries, just bring it back to room temperature before using or serving.

Some of the other flavours I use to coat the labneh include: rosemary, thyme, crushed walnuts, crushed pistachios, sesame seeds, za'atar, mint, dill and sumac.

***Tip** Use the flavoured oil in salad dressings or for cooking!*

Easy Crostini

Combine two recipes to make an easy and tasty third? Winning! All of the components can be made in advance for easy serving when your guests arrive. Or arrange everything on a platter and let them help themselves! Sweet onions, woody thyme and a creamy feta cheese that you'll want to spread on everything.

Ingredients

1 stale loaf or baguette, cut into thin slices
2 tbsp olive oil
½ cup caramelised onions, see page 21
1 quantity Mediterranean baked feta, see page 101
80g prosciutto, sliced
2 sprigs fresh thyme

***Makes** 8–10 serves as an appetiser*
***Takes** 25 minutes*

Method

Preheat oven to 160°C.

Toss the bread slices in the olive oil and spread out on a lined oven tray. Season with salt and freshly ground black pepper. Bake for 15–20 minutes, until crispy and lightly golden. These can be made ahead and stored in an airtight container for up to 2 weeks.

To assemble, spread each toast with some caramelised onion. Top with a spoonful of baked feta and a roasted tomato. Finish with a ribbon of prosciutto and a couple of fresh thyme leaves.

***Tip** Skip the Mediterranean Baked Feta step and substitute with 200g fresh feta cheese or goats' cheese and 100g ripe cherry tomatoes, sliced in half.*

Tomato Confit

Confit is an old technique where meat is preserved in its own fat. The most well-known dish is the French duck confit – here we use the same fancy term to slowly poach and preserve tomatoes in olive oil. If you're lucky enough to have homegrown tomatoes, wait until they're ripe and bursting with flavour and sunshine and then stock your fridge with these beauties – they'll hold their shape and ooze with intense sweetness.

Ingredients

500g tomatoes
3 garlic cloves, skin on
2–3 bay leaves
1 tsp salt
2 cups olive oil

Makes *2 cups*
Takes *2 hours*

Dairy-free | Gluten-free

Method

Preheat oven to 130°C.

Arrange the tomatoes, garlic and bay leaves in a small baking dish. Sprinkle over salt and drizzle over olive oil until the tomatoes are two-thirds submerged.

Bake for 1 ½–2 hours until the tomatoes are wrinkled but still holding their shape. Remove from the oven and cool in the oil to room temperature.

Transfer tomatoes to an airtight container and pour over the cooking oil so they are completely covered (top up with extra olive oil if necessary). Store in the fridge for up to two weeks.

Tip *Jazz up a salad, toss through a summery pasta, serve alongside barbecued meats or simply spread these confit tomatoes straight onto your toast!*

Garlic Confit & Garlic Bread

Confit garlic cloves are unctuously soft and sweet, and at the same time you'll produce an aromatic oil that can be used for a whole host of other purposes. Confit garlic and Parmesan will take your garlic bread to a whole new level ... Eat them as-is for the ultimate appetiser or serve alongside your favourite soup for a warming and decadent everyday meal.

Ingredients

2 whole heads of garlic
2–3 bay leaves
1 tsp salt
1 cup olive oil
2 tsp oregano, finely chopped
½ tsp dried chilli flakes
1 tbsp butter
1 cup Parmesan, grated
1 day-old baguette

Makes *4 serves*
Takes *1 hour*

Method

Peel the garlic cloves and place them in a small saucepan, along with the bay leaves and salt. Add the oil, bring it to a very gentle simmer and then reduce the heat as low as it can go. Poach the garlic in the just-simmering oil for 45 minutes to 1 hour, until the garlic is soft but not falling apart.

Place the garlic cloves in a clean jar and top with the oil so they are fully submerged. Cool to room temperature before sealing the jar and storing in the fridge. The confit cloves will keep for 2–3 weeks in the refrigerator.

To make the garlic bread, preheat grill to 200°C. Place 8–10 cloves of confit garlic in a small bowl and mash to a paste with the back of a fork. Add oregano, chilli flakes, butter and Parmesan. Mix well, and season with salt and freshly ground black pepper.

Slice baguette on an angle into thin slices. Grill for 2 minutes, watching carefully, flip over and grill the other side for 2 more minutes. Remove from the oven, spread each slice with garlic paste and then grill for 2 more minutes, until the cheese is golden and bubbling. Serve immediately.

Tip *How to use your garlic confit:*

- *Whisk a few cloves and some of the oil with fresh lemon juice to make a simple vinaigrette*
- *Smash some garlic confit cloves and toss through steamed veges with a drizzle of the garlic oil*
- *Mix mashed garlic confit with some butter and slip it under the skin of a chicken before roasting*
- *Mash a few cloves and toss through diced tomatoes and fresh basil and pile on top of fresh bread for a delicious bruschetta snack.*

Tuna Confit

If you can get your hands on some fresh tuna steaks, this recipe is so simple and you'll never have to reach for the canned variety again. Confit tuna has a lovely melting texture, as the fish is essentially slow-poached in olive oil without absorbing the fat. You can serve it warm or cold — your niçoise salad has never tasted so good!

Ingredients

1 tbsp salt
½ tsp caster sugar
500g fresh tuna
1–2 bay leaves
8 whole black peppercorns
1 lemon
2 cups olive oil

Makes *4–6 serves*
Takes *40 minutes*

Gluten-free | Dairy-free

Method

Mix together the salt and sugar and rub is all over the tuna. Place in a small saucepan and cover with olive oil so the tuna is completely submerged.

Add bay leaves, peppercorns and long curls of lemon zest. Don't waste the zested lemon, slice it into rounds and add 2-3 slices to the oil, too.

Place the saucepan on low heat and gently warm the olive oil through until it's barely simmering. Cook for 15–20 minutes, depending on the size and thickness of your tuna — it should change colour but still retain some softness. Remove from the heat.

Let the tuna cool in the oil for 15 minutes. Transfer tuna to an airtight container, strain the olive oil through a fine sieve to remove the herbs and lemon peel, and pour over tuna so it's completely covered (top up with extra olive oil if necessary). Store in the fridge for up to two weeks.

Tip *Choose a saucepan that is only slightly larger than the tuna your confiting, so you don't have to use unnecessary amounts of olive oil to cover the fish.*

Corned Beef Balls

Leftovers become epic party favours with these corned beef balls, although who needs the excuse of a party to whip these up as a tasty appetiser — less waste and delicious to boot! You don't need a lot of corned beef so it's a great cost-stretcher. You could roll larger balls as serve them as a family-friendly dinner option, too.

Ingredients

2 cups leftover potatoes, roughly mashed
½ cup leftover corned beef, shredded
½ cup mozzarella cheese, grated
2–3 large cornichons, finely chopped
2 eggs
½ cup flour
2 cups panko breadcrumbs
vegetable oil

Makes *16 balls*
Takes *20 minutes plus chilling time*

Gluten-free / Dairy-free

Method

In a medium bowl, mix together potatoes, corned beef, mozzarella and cornichons and 1 egg. Season with salt and freshly ground black pepper. Roll into ping-pong-sized balls.

Take 3 small shallow bowls. In one add flour and season with salt and freshly ground black pepper. In the second, add the remaining egg and whisk together with 2 tbsp water. In the third, add panko breadcrumbs.

Taking one ball at a time, roll it in flour, dip it in egg, and then roll it in crumbs. Place the crumbed balls on a plate and continue until all of the balls are coated. Refrigerate for 15 minutes to firm up.

Heat oil in a frying pan or saucepan over a medium heat until shimmering. Add the balls one by one, taking care not to overcrowd the pan. You may need to cook them in 2 batches. Flip the balls several times as they're coking then remove them from the pan once they're golden brown, 4–5 minutes. Drain on a paper towel-lined plate.

Serve with mayo and a dollop of homemade pesto, see page 40.

Tip *Make these slightly healthier by forming into patties, pan-frying with a little oil and then finishing off in the oven.*

Leftover Roast Beef Sarnie

I love a hot roast dinner but for me, a roast really comes into its own when leftovers are involved. Paper-thin ribbons of sirloin steak are sandwiched inside a fresh baguette with caramelised onions, Dijon mayo, homemade bread & butter pickles and salad greens — no scrimping on condiments for the tastiest sarnie you've had in months.

Ingredients

1 fresh baguette
½ cup caramelised onions, see page 21
½ cup mayonnaise
2 tbsp Dijon mustard
2 handfuls salad greens
200g leftover sirloin steak, thinly sliced
¼ cup bread & butter pickles, see page 14

Makes *4 serves*
Takes *10 minutes*

Method

Slice baguette lengthways. Spread one half with caramelised onions.

In a small bowl, mix together mayonnaise and Dijon mustard. Spread over the other half of the baguette.

Layer salad greens, sirloin beef and bread & butter pickles evenly along the length of the baguette. Season with salt and freshly ground black pepper.

Divide the baguette into four and serve.

Tip *Leave out the salad greens and add some slices of Gruyère cheese and grill this sandwich in the oven for 3–4 minutes for the ultimate roast beef toastie.*

Pot Roast & Kimchi Reuben

Use your pot roast leftovers to make this moreish sandwich for lunch the next day. A great Reuben sandwich is salty, tangy and creamy all at the same time. Here I use homemade kimchi and Sriracha mayo for a spicy twist, but you can use whatever pickles or condiments you have on hand. A traditional Reuben would be served with mustard, sauerkraut and Russian dressing.

Ingredients

½ cup mayonnaise
1 tsp Worcestershire sauce
1 tbsp Sriracha sauce
8 slices bread, toasted
400g leftover corned beef, see page 182
8 slices Swiss cheese
8 tbsp kimchi, see page 17
Handful fresh coriander leaves

Makes *4 sandwiches*
Takes *10 minutes*

Method

To make the Sriracha mayo, combine mayonnaise, Worcestershire sauce and Sriracha sauce in a small bowl.

Spread Sriracha mayo evenly over half of the toasted bread.

Arrange beef, cheese, kimchi and coriander leaves evenly across the 4 slices. Top with the remaining 4 slices of bread

Tip *Grill and serve hot for extra deliciousness!*

Salad Bar

With an almost infinite number of combinations, salads are the very core of our daily JUK cabinet — use your imagination to try out new textures and flavours.

Szechuan Cucumber Salad

This is a simple salad but so numbingly cleansing and pleasing on the palate. The longer you marinade the cucumbers for, the more flavor they'll absorb. But don't pickle them for too long as you want them to retain a nice crisp texture. Serve as a side with dumplings or your favourite Chinese-inspired dishes. You can also add coriander and toasted peanuts at the end for extra texture.

Ingredients

2 cucumbers
1 tsp salt
3 garlic cloves, crushed
1 tsp sugar
1 tbsp light soy sauce
1 tbsp rice vinegar
2 tbsp Szechuan oil, see recipe page 122 or sesame oil plus ½ tsp Szechuan peppercorns
Chilli flakes, to taste
1 spring onion, thinly sliced
1 fresh red chilli, thinly sliced
1 tsp white sesame seeds
1 tsp black sesame seeds

***Makes** 4–6 serves as a side dish*
***Takes** 10 minutes*

Dairy-free

Method

Cut the cucumbers in quarters lengthwise, and remove the seedy middle section. Cut each quarter into bite-sized chunks. Sprinkle with salt and place in a colander over the sink for 10 minutes, to draw out excess moisture.

Meanwhile in a small bowl, mix together garlic, sugar, soy sauce, rice vinegar and Szechuan oil, plus chilli flakes to taste. If you're not using pre-made Szechuan oil, heat sesame oil in a small frying pan over medium heat until hot. Smash the peppercorns with the flat of your knife and add to the hot pan. Cook until they smell fragrant and are toasted but not burned. Pour into the small bowl immediately and mix with the other ingredients. Set aside.

In a small dry frying pan, toast the sesame seeds until fragrant and lightly browned. Set aside.

Pat the cucumbers dry with a paper towel and toss them in the Szechuan dressing, mixing well. Place onto a serving plate and top with spring onion, fresh red chilli and toasted sesame seeds.

Szechuan Oil

My Szechuan oil recipe from My Underground Deli *is included below if you don't already own a copy of my second cookbook — I drizzle this on EVERYTHING! The flavour of Szechuan pepper is more numbing than spicy, and combined with aromatics like star anise, chilli and cardamom, there's no wonder it's so moreish.*

Ingredients

500ml canola oil
1 whole head of garlic
10cm nub of ginger, sliced
10 star anise
5 cinnamon quills
5 cardamom pods
¼ cup dried whole chillies
½ cup Szechuan peppercorns
1 tsp salt
2 tbsp soy sauce

Makes *2 cups*
Takes *2 ¼ hours cooking time for oil plus overnight resting*

Dairy-free

Method

Heat oil in a heavy-bottomed saucepan over very low heat. Add the garlic, ginger, star anise, cinnamon, coriander seeds and cardamom pods to the oil and simmer, making sure the garlic and ginger doesn't burn, for at least 2 hours, until the oil is very fragrant. Add the dried chillies and Szechuan peppercorns and simmer for another 10 minutes. Remove from the heat and add salt and soy sauce. Cover and allow the oil to cool completely overnight.

Once cooled, pour into clean, sterilised jars and keep in the fridge until needed.

Tip *You can keep the aromatics sitting in the oil and the flavour will develop even more over time. Drain oil through a fine sieve as needed.*

Chinese
Cabbage

Summer Melon & Cucumber Salad

This fresh, seasonal salad is delicious for breakfast, lunch or dinner! With a rosewater-spiked labneh and toasted za'atar spice mix (which is amazing to have on hand for a whole bunch of dishes, so make extra) the natural sweetness of the melons really takes centre stage. Keep your melons and cucumbers chilled for an extra-refreshing option on a hot summer's day.

Ingredients

Za'atar spice mix

2 tbsp sesame seeds, toasted
1 tbsp ground cumin
1 tbsp ground coriander
1 tbsp sumac
1 tsp dried thyme
1 tsp flaky sea salt

Salad

1 cup labneh, *see page 44*
1-2 tsp rosewater, to taste
3-4 Persian cucumbers
½ rockmelon
½ honeydew melon
1 lemon, zested and juiced
1 tsp honey
2 tbsp good quality olive oil
Small handful fennel fronds, or dill

Makes *4 serves*
Takes *10 minutes*

Method

To make the za'atar spice mix, combine all of the ingredients in a small bowl. You can store this mixture in an airtight container for up to two weeks.

In a small bowl, fold rosewater through the labneh.

Roughly chop the cucumbers. Peel, deseed and roughly chop the melons. Place in a medium-sized bowl and toss with lemon zest, lemon juice, honey and olive oil. Season with salt and freshly ground black pepper.

Spread the labneh on a plate, top with the melon mixture and dust with za'atar. Top with fennel fronds to serve.

Rainbow Israeli Salad

When summer produce is at its best, this simple salsa-esque chopped salad is the perfect accompaniment for grilled fish, barbecued meats, rice dishes and more. Serve it with thick, creamy hummus and pita breads for a fresh, healthy snack, or toss it through cooked bulghur wheat or quinoa for a more substantial salad.

Ingredients

3 firm tomatoes
1 red capsicum
1 yellow capsicum
2 Lebanese cucumbers, or 1 telegraph cucumber with the seedy middle section removed
4–5 small radishes
1 small red onion
½ pomegranate, deseeded
½ cup parsley, finely chopped
½ cup coriander, finely chopped
1 lemon, zested & juiced
2 tbsp extra virgin olive oil
1 tsp sumac

Makes *4–6 serves as a side dish*
Takes *15 minutes*

Gluten-free | Dairy-free | Vegan

Method

Quarter the tomatoes and remove the seeds. Quarter the capsicums and remove the seeds. Finely dice the tomatoes, capsicums, cucumbers and radishes into evenly-sized pieces. Peel the red onion and finely dice.

Place the diced ingredients into a bowl and add the pomegranate arils, parsley, coriander, lemon zest, lemon juice, olive oil and sumac. Mix well to combine. Season with salt and pepper to taste. Add more lemon juice if needed. Serve immediately.

Tip *A rough chop will make this salad more rustic!*

Bacon, Walnut & Roasted Radish Salad

We don't champion the humble radish nearly enough here in New Zealand. They taste like spring — cool, sharp and slightly peppery — I adore them dipped raw into hummus. Roasted radishes are the hero in this salad, which is a fun way to play with them when you still want a heartier salad. And I don't need to sell you on bacon and candied walnuts...

Ingredients

2 bunches radishes, ends trimmed and quartered lengthways
8–10 cloves garlic, skin on
1 tbsp olive oil
4 rashers streaky bacon, diced
½ cup walnut halves
2 tbsp brown sugar
1 tbsp butter
100g mixed green & red salad leaves
4 pickled eggs, see page 98

***Makes** 4 serves*
***Takes** 30 minutes*

Gluten-free | Dairy-free

Method

Preheat oven to 180°C. Toss radishes and garlic cloves in olive oil and spread on a lined baking tray. Season generously with salt and freshly ground black pepper. Roast for 20 minutes, until lightly browned but still retaining some firmness. Set aside to cool slightly.

Heat a non-stick frying pan over medium heat and cook off the bacon for 2–3 minutes until nicely browned. Remove from the pan and set aside on some paper towel.

Use the same frying pan to candy your walnuts. Heat walnuts, sugar and butter over medium heat, stirring continuously, for around 5 minutes until the sugar is melted and the nuts are coated. Transfer immediately onto a sheet of baking paper and separate the nuts using two spatulas (you'll need to do this quickly so they don't stick together in large clumps). Be careful not to burn yourself with the molten sugar. Leave for 5–7 minutes for the sugar coating to harden.

In a large bowl or serving platter, layer salad leaves, roasted radishes, bacon and candied walnuts. Top with halved pickled eggs and drizzle with a decent glug of extra virgin olive oil (it's all this salad needs). Serve with an extra crack or two of black pepper, to taste.

***Tip** If your radishes have nice, fresh leaves, save them to toss through the salad at the end for a peppery, almost rocket-like punch.*

Carrot, Goats' Cheese & Pine Nut Salad

One thing I've noticed, the more I've been involved with food, is that it's now the simple things that impress me the most. This salad is a celebration of carrots — all different shapes and colours, ribboned and pulled together with a fabulous roasted capsicum harissa dressing. Pine nuts for crunch, goats' cheese for creaminess, parsley for herbaciousness. You don't need anything else!

Ingredients

½ cup pine nuts
4 large carrots, different colours if you can find them
1 cup harissa dressing, *see page 57*
100g goats' cheese, crumbled
Handful parsley leaves

Makes *4 serves*
Takes *10 minutes*

Gluten-free | Dairy-free

Method

Place a small dry frying pan over medium heat and toast off the pine nuts for 2–3 minutes, until fragrant and slightly browned. Set aside to cool.

Using a vegetable peeler, peel long lengths of carrot into ribbons.

Swirl the harissa dressing generously across the bottom of a large plate or bowl. Place the carrot ribbons on top of the dressing. Scatter over the pine nuts, goats' cheese and parsley. Season with salt and freshly ground black pepper before serving.

Tip *If you're not serving the salad straight away, you can ribbon the carrots in advance and store them in a container covered with cold water in the fridge. They'll stay firm and crisp in the water. Drain well before serving.*

Serve with roast lamb or beef, or as part of a Middle Eastern-inpsired spread.

Beetroot, Citrus & Avocado Salad

This salad is so fresh and bright — I don't often serve whole slices of lemon and lime in a salad but the intensity works against the earthiness of the beetroot and the creaminess of the avocado and the tahini dressing. If you take the time to slice each component you'll be rewarded with a colourful showstopper of a salad.

Ingredients

2 oranges, peeled
2 grapefruits, peeled
1 lemon, peeled
1 lime, peeled
2–3 beetroot, mixed colours if you can find them
1 avocado
½ cup tahini jar dressing, see recipe page 58
Handful fennel fronds, to garnish
Pinch sea salt

Makes *4 serves*
Takes *15 minutes*

Gluten-free | Dairy-free | Vegan

Method

Carefully slice the orange, grapefruit, lemon and lime into thin rounds. Peel the beetroot and use a mandolin to slice into super thin wafers. Halve and slice the avocado.

Arrange the sliced ingredients on a large platter and drizzle with tahini dressing. Sprinkle with fennel fronds and sea salt just before serving.

Tip *Whether they're grated or thinly shaved, beetroots are wonderful to eat raw — they have a crunchy texture with a strong earthy flavour. Chioggia beets have a gorgeous striped pattern on the inside, which is lost when they're cooked, so save these beauties for salads and garnishes.*

Lighter Tomato & Tuna Niçoise Salad

A salad to champion your lush confit tomatoes and tuna! With creamy mozzarella, salty capers and Kalamata olives, this is a statement salad and made even more tastier thanks to the extra effort of confiting your own tuna and tomatoes. Although obviously a can of tuna and fresh tomatoes work as stand-ins here, too.

Ingredients

100g green beans
50g mesclun leaves
½ cup Kalamata olives
½ small red onion, finely sliced
1 tbsp capers
125g fresh mozzarella
4 confit vine tomatoes, or fresh tomatoes
200g confit tuna, or canned tuna
2 tbsp reserved oil from the confit tomatoes, or olive oil
2 tbsp red wine vinegar
Handful fresh basil leaves
1 tsp dried chilli flakes
Fresh lemon, to serve

Makes *4 serves*
Takes *15 minutes*

Gluten-free

Method

Bring a small saucepan of water to the boil. Top and tail the green beans and add to the pot with a pinch of salt. Cook for 2–3 minutes until just blanched. Drain and refresh in ice-cold water. Put to one side.

Divide the mesclun between four plates. Top with olives, red onion, capers, torn mozzarella, tomatoes and tuna. Drizzle over oil and red wine vinegar. Finish with a scattering of fresh basil leaves and chilli flakes. Season with salt and freshly ground black pepper, and serve with a cheek of lemon on the side.

Tip *Beef up your salad niçoise by adding in the traditional hard-boiled eggs, potatoes and anchovies.*

Persian Rice Salad

This is not your average rice salad. We made it for a Middle-Eastern inspired wedding feast and it's been on rotation on our menus ever since. Every mouthful is peppered with fruits, nuts and spices. Delicious served as part of a spread or simply with a fried egg on top for an easy lunch or dinner.

Ingredients

2 cups long grain rice
½ cup sultanas
½ cup golden raisins
½ cup dried currants
½ cup dried cranberries
½ cup sliced almonds, toasted
½ cup chopped pistachios, toasted
2 tbsp sesame seeds, toasted
1 carrot, peeled & grated
Handful coriander leaves
Pinch saffron threads, soaked in 3 tbsp hot water for 5 minutes
¼ cup olive oil
1 lemon, zested & juiced
1 orange, zested & juiced
2 tsp honey
½ tsp ground cinnamon
2 tbsp fresh pomegranate arils
1 tbsp dried rose petals

Makes *6–8 serves*
Takes *45 minutes*

Gluten-free | Dairy-free | Vegan

Method

Cook rice according to packet instructions. Remove from the pot, spread out rice in a large shallow dish and allow to cool.

In a large bowl, toss together sultanas, raisins, currants, cranberries, almonds, pistachios, sesame seeds, carrot, coriander and cooled rice.

Whisk together saffron threads and water, oil, lemon zest and juice, orange zest and juice, honey and cinnamon. Pour over rice and toss to coat. Season to taste with salt and freshly ground black pepper.

Serve with fresh coriander leaves, pomegranate arils and dried rose petals.

Tip *Don't worry if you don't have every single ingredient listed above – it's supposed to be over-the-top opulent. You can do a simplified version or add your own favourite dried fruit or nuts.*

Everyday Meals

The busy working week often leaves us short on energy and inspiration — but with a little foresight you'll be whipping up these fresh & easy eats in no time.

JB's Fish Larb

I'm a big fan of a Thai larb salad and often make it with chicken or pork, so when my friend JB told me she was cooking a fish larb for dinner I was initially puzzled... but ultimately pleasantly surprised! It's fresh, full of zingy flavours and easy to prep in advance. Served here with coconut rice but also fabulous spooned into lettuce cups for Asian 'tacos'.

Ingredients

1 cup jasmine rice
1 cup coconut milk
400g white fish fillets, skinless & boneless
200g green beans, sliced into small rounds
1 cup mint leaves
1 cup coriander, leaves picked and stalks reserved
2 kaffir lime leaves, finely chopped
3 tbsp fish sauce
2 tbsp soy sauce
1–2 stalks lemongrass, finely chopped
2cm thumb fresh ginger, peeled and grated
1 small red chilli, seeds removed and finely sliced
2 tbsp lime juice
1 romaine or cos lettuce
1 carrot, peeled
2 baby cucumbers
1 tbsp sesame oil
2 tbsp toasted peanuts
2 tbsp crispy shallots

Makes *4 serves*
Takes *20 minutes*

Method

Place rice, coconut milk and ½ cup of water in a medium saucepan over medium heat. Cover, bring to a gentle simmer and cook for 12 minutes. Remove from the heat, leave covered and steam for a further 10 minutes.

Finely dice the fish, so you're almost mincing it. Place diced fish in a medium bowl.

To the bowl, add beans, half of the mint finely chopped, coriander stalks finely chopped, kaffir lime, fish sauce, soy sauce, lemongrass, ginger, chilli and lemon or lime juice. Stir well to coat the fish. Cover and place in the fridge for 10 minutes to marinate.

Meanwhile, prepare the other ingredients. Wash and dry the cos lettuce leaves, julienne the carrot and slice the cucumbers.

Heat sesame oil in a medium frying pan over medium heat. Add the fish mix to the pan and cook, stirring, occasionally, for 2–3 minutes until the fish is just cooked through.

Divide the rice between four bowls. Top with the larb mix, dividing the cooking juices evenly between the bowls. Top with reserved mint leaves, coriander leaves, peanuts and crispy shallots.

Serve with extra fish sauce, chilli and lemon or lime wedges on the side, so people can add extra to taste.

Tip *Look for gluten-free soy sauce or tamari to keep this meal gluten-free.*

Thai Green Curry Paste

There is always a time and a place for store-bought curry pastes, and I have a variety of different jars on hand in my fridge at home. But if you really want to add the wow factor to your dinner, take the time to make this paste from scratch. You'll taste the difference, I promise! Adjust the chilli quantities to suit your taste.

Ingredients

4–6 fresh green chillies, roughly chopped
6 garlic cloves, peeled
2cm piece galangal (or fresh ginger), finely chopped
¼ red onion, chopped, or a small shallot
Handful fresh coriander, stalks and roots attached
2 stalks lemongrass, outer leaves removed and finely chopped
1 lime, zested & grated
8 kaffir lime leaves, torn into pieces
1 tsp ground cumin
1 tbsp coriander seeds
2 tsp soy sauce
¼ cup water, as needed to loosen
4 tbsp vegetable oil

Makes *1 cup*
Takes *15 minutes*

Gluten-free | Dairy-free | Vegan

Method

Place all of the ingredients in a blender except for the water and oil and blitz to a smooth paste. Add water if needed to break down the ingredients into a paste.

Heat the oil in a medium-sized saucepan and gently fry the paste for 8–10 minutes.

Spoon into a jar and store for up to 2 weeks in the fridge.

Tip *At work I make my curry pastes fish- and shellfish-free to keep them vegan, but you can add 1 tbsp of fish sauce to really make this curry sing!*

Thai Green Chicken Curry

Did you know that Thai green chicken curry was the first meal I served on the Underground Kitchen menu, ever? Back when I cooked from my little pink house in Ponsonby, with no dishwasher and a tiny menu I posted on Facebook every week! This curry is light and healthy and you can add whatever fresh greens you have on hand.

Ingredients

1 tbsp olive oil
400g chicken breast, diced
1x 400ml can coconut milk
3 tbsp green curry paste, see page 146
4 kaffir lime leaves
½ eggplant, diced
1 tbsp fish sauce
1 tbsp lime juice
1 tbsp sugar
2 bok choy, roughly chopped into bite-sized lengths
4–6 stems broccolini, roughly chopped into bite-sized lengths
1 tbsp sesame oil
Handful fresh coriander leaves
Handful fresh bean sprouts
2 tbsp crispy shallots

Makes *4 serves*
Takes *20 minutes*

Method

Heat the oil in a medium-sized saucepan and gently fry the chicken for 4–5 minutes, until cooked through. Remove chicken from the pan and place to one side.

With the same saucepan on the stove, add the coconut milk and curry paste and stir well to combine. Cook for 5 minutes, until the oils start to rise to the surface. Add the kaffir lime leaves and eggplant and cook for 3–4 minutes until the eggplant is just cooked.

Add the fish sauce, lime juice, sugar, bok choy and broccolini and cook 2 more minutes, until the greens are just cooked. Add chicken back to the pan and stir to coat. Remove from the heat.

Taste and add more lime juice (for sourness) or sugar (for sweetness) as necessary. Drizzle over sesame oil and top with coriander leaves, bean sprouts and crispy shallots.

Serve with steamed jasmine rice.

Tip *If you've got leftover roast chicken or cooked chicken breast, shred it and add it at the end instead of cooking chicken for an even quicker and easier everyday meal.*

Vietnamese Caramel Salmon

The salty-sweet South-East Asian caramel flavour pairs beautifully with the richness of the salmon and the sourness of the lime in this quick and easy noodle dish. Add freshness with seasonal greens and you've got yourself a winning everyday meal — any leftovers will be great for lunch the following day, too. Serve with steamed jasmine rice as an alternative to rice noodles.

Ingredients

½ cup sugar
¼ cup water
2 tbsp fish sauce
100g broccolini, or other seasonal greens
¼ cup cracked black pepper
400g fresh salmon, skin on and pin-boned, cut into 4 even-sized fillets
2 tbsp sesame oil
300g wide rice noodles
2 kaffir lime leaves, finely sliced
Handful coriander leaves
2 spring onions, finely chopped
1 fresh red chilli, seeds removed and finely chopped
Lime wedges, to serve

***Makes** 4 serves*
***Takes** 25 minutes*

Gluten-free | Dairy-free

Method

To make the Vietnamese caramel, place the sugar and water in a small saucepan over medium heat, Boil, without stirring, until it turns a light golden brown, swirling the pan every once in a while to ensure the colour is even. Remove from the heat and add 2 more tablespoons of water and the fish sauce (it'll bubble furiously and darken in colour). Once the caramel has stopped bubbling, mix well and allow to cool.

Bring a small saucepan of water to the boil. Trim broccolini and add to the pot with a pinch of salt. Cook for 2–3 minutes until just blanched. Drain and refresh in ice-cold water. Put to one side.

Place the pepper on a plate and press the salmon flesh-side down into the pepper to coat the flesh.

Heat a large non-stick frying pan over a medium-high heat. Add 1 tablespoon sesame oil and place the salmon fillets pepper-side down in the pan. Cook for 3 minutes before turning skin-side down and cook for 5 more minutes or until just cooked through.

Meanwhile, bring a large saucepan of boiling water to the boil. Cook rice noodles according to packet instructions. Drain and toss with remaining sesame oil.

Divide the noodles between 4 bowls and top each bowl with a piece of salmon, some broccolini and a generous drizzle of caramel. Scatter over kaffir lime, coriander, spring onion, fresh chilli and serve with lime wedges.

Cook's Note

You can keep this dairy-free by using coconut cream instead of cow's cream, just balance the flavours with salt, pepper and lemon juice to taste.

Harry's Mushroom Stroganoff with Plenty of Greens

I love a hearty stroganoff and this quick, meat-free version is perfect for an everyday meal. I like to add lots of leafy greens for extra nutrition and I can confirm that this dinner tastes even better the next day — so plan for leftovers! You can experiment with different types of mushrooms to find your perfect combo.

Ingredients

250g fettuccine
2 tbsp olive oil
300g Portobello mushrooms, or your favourite mushroom combo
1 onion, finely sliced
3 cloves garlic, finely diced
1 tbsp soy sauce
1 tbsp Dijon mustard
1 tbsp Worcestershire sauce (vegetarian)
¼ tsp cayenne pepper
1 tbsp lemon juice
1 ½ cups cream
150g cavalo nero, kale or other leafy greens
1 egg
½ cup shaved Parmesan, to serve

Makes *4 serves*
Takes *20 minutes*

Method

Cook fettuccine according to packet instructions. Drain, and keep to one side.

In a large saucepan, heat olive oil over medium-high heat. Add mushrooms and sauté for 5 minutes. Add onion and cook for another 2-3 minutes, until the onions are transparent. Add garlic and soy sauce and cook for a further minute.

Add Dijon mustard, Worcestershire sauce, cayenne pepper, lemon juice and cream. Reduce heat to low and cook for 5 minutes. Season with salt and freshly ground black pepper. Remove pan from heat.

Add egg and whisk through, until sauce is silky and slightly thickened. Add cavalo nero and stir through to wilt.

Add cooked pasta to the pan and gently toss through the sauce.

Spoon into a serving bowl and finish with a sprinkling of Parmesan.

Tip *Adding the egg at the end helps to emulsify and add richness to the stroganoff sauce — but whatever you do, don't add it while the pan is still on the stove or your eggs will scramble!*

Mexican Beef & Black Bean Meatballs

Rich and warming, these meatballs are a delicious year-round meal. If you're gluten-free, substitute the fresh breadcrumbs in the meatballs with ½ cup cooked quinoa — you'll get the same moistness and lightness but without the gluten. Roll the meatballs ahead of time and free-flow freeze them so they're ready to go during the week; all you'll need to do is make the sauce and cook them through.

Ingredients

600g beef mince
1 egg
1 cup fresh breadcrumbs
1 tsp ground cumin
1 tsp ground coriander
½ tsp smoked paprika
¼ tsp cayenne pepper
½ tsp salt
Small handful fresh coriander leaves, finely chopped
3 tbsp olive oil
1 red onion, finely diced
2 cloves garlic, crushed
1x 400g can chopped tomatoes
2 tbsp balsamic vinegar
2 tbsp chipotle sauce
1 tbsp brown sugar
1 tsp ground cumin
1 tsp ground coriander
1 tsp ground cinnamon
½ tsp chilli flakes
1x 400g can black beans, drained

Fresh coriander sauce

1 small green chilli, seeds removed and finely chopped
Large handful coriander leaves
2 tbsp lemon juice
4 tbsp vegetable oil

***Makes** 4 serves*
***Takes** 25 minutes*

Method

To make the meatballs, combine the mince, egg, breadcrumbs, spices, salt and fresh coriander in a bowl. Roll into golf-sized balls.

Heat 1 tablespoon of the olive oil in a large frying pan and brown the meatballs. Transfer to a plate and set aside.

Add the onion and garlic to the same pan and cook for 2–3 minutes until translucent. Add the tomatoes, ½ cup water, balsamic vinegar, chipotle sauce, sugar, cumin, coriander, cinnamon and chilli flakes. Season with salt and freshly ground black pepper.

Carefully add the meatballs back to the sauce, nestling them into the liquid, and simmer gently for 8–10 minutes until the meatballs are cooked through.

Add the black beans to the sauce and stir through.

To make the fresh coriander sauce, place coriander, chilli and lemon juice in a blender and blend until you have a smooth paste. Season with salt and freshly ground black pepper to taste.

Serve the meatballs on a bed of rice with dollops of sour cream and fresh coriander sauce.

***Tip** Have a wrap night party and serve these meatballs along with all of your favourite condiments in the centre of the table — everyone can build their own Mexican meatball wraps.*

My favourite brand of chipotle sauce is La Morena — you can find it in a small orange can in the specialties aisle of your supermarket.

Korean Beef Short Rib Tacos

I love this Asian twist on tacos — the beef is melt-in-your-mouth tender with heaps of flavour, and the zingy apple & radish salsa cuts through the richness of the short rib. Serve everything in bowls on the table, so people can build their own tacos. Go easy on the chilli sauce if you're feeding the kids. Turn this into a vege option with slow-cooked jackfruit (and omit the fish sauce) — it has a great texture for tacos.

Ingredients

Slow-cooked ribs

800g beef short rib, bone in
6 cloves garlic, smashed
Thumb-sized knob of ginger, peeled & grated
1 pear, cored & grated
½ cup soy sauce
½ cup brown sugar
2 tbsp sriracha sauce
6 tbsp rice wine vinegar
2 tbsp fish sauce
2 tbsp sesame oil

Salsa

1 granny smith apple
4 radishes
2 spring onions
1 lemon, zested & juiced
1 tsp sesame seeds, toasted
Handful mint, finely chopped

To serve

12 6" tortilla wraps, mayonnaise, Sriracha sauce and lemon wedges

Makes *4 serves*
Takes *4 hours or 10 hours*

Method

To prepare the short ribs, whisk together garlic, ginger, pear, soy sauce, sugar, sriracha, rice wine vinegar, fish sauce and sesame oil. Place beef in a bowl and pour over marinade, turning to coat. Cover and chill overnight to marinate (optional).

To use a slow cooker: place beef in the slow cooker and pour over marinade. Cover and cook on low for 8–10 hours, or until tender.

To cook in the oven: preheat Preheat oven to 160°C. Place beef in an ovenproof dish and pour over the marinade plus 1 cup water. Cover and cook for 3–4 hours, until tender. Turn several times to coat in the sauce and add extra water if the dish is drying out.

Remove from the slow cooker or oven and shred the beef with two forks. Remove the bones, toss through the sauce and set to one side.

To make the salsa, julienne the apple, radishes and spring onions, and toss all of the ingredients together in a bowl. Season with salt and freshly ground black pepper.

Heat tortillas in the microwave or a dry frying pan. Serve warmed tortillas with mayonnaise, Sriracha sauce, apple salsa, pulled beef short rib and extra lemon wedges for squeezing over.

Best Bologneseiov

This is the base I use for my beef & mozzarella lasagne, and it's packed with so much flavour. Serve with your favourite pasta, on toast or even in a pie. It's a great meal to make ahead and freeze for nights when you don't have time (or energy) to cook. And be sure to cook extra so you can make my leftover Breakfast Bolognese Bowl, see page 77.

Ingredients

2 tbsp olive oil
2 onions, diced
4 cloves garlic, crushed
600g good-quality beef mince
50g tomato paste
1x 400g can chopped tomatoes
1 cup beef stock
2 tbsp Worcestershire sauce
2 tbsp balsamic vinegar
1 tsp Marmite (optional)
2 tbsp brown sugar
2 tbsp ground cumin
1 tbsp ground coriander
2 tsp ground cinnamon
2 tbsp dried mixed herbs
1 tsp dried chilli flakes
1 tsp smoked paprika
2 bay leaves

Makes *6 serves*
Takes *40 minutes*

Gluten-free | Dairy-free

Method

Heat the olive oil in a large, heavy-based saucepan. Add the onion and a pinch of salt and cook, for 3–4 minutes until translucent, stirring occasionally. Add the garlic and cook for another 2 minutes.

Push the onion and garlic to one side of the pan and add the mince. Cook, stirring with a wooden spoon to break up the mince, for about 8 minutes or until well browned. Add the tomato paste and cook for another minute. Add the remaining ingredients and stir well.

Bring to the boil, then reduce heat to low. Simmer, uncovered, for about 30 minutes or until the sauce has thickened. Season with salt and freshly ground black pepper. Carefully remove the bay leaves and take off the heat.

Tip *I sometimes add a tablespoon of fish sauce instead of Marmite, because it brings so much umami (the fifth flavour pillar) and depth to the sauce! Fish sauce is not just for Asian cooking...*

Okonomiyaki

These Japanese pancakes are quick, simple and satisfying, and a great way to use up leftover proteins or veggies. The recipe is for one pancake so you can easily scale it, depending how many people you're feeding. I went to a restaurant in Tokyo where they brought out all the raw ingredients to your table, which housed a large grill, and you mixed & cooked your own okonomiyaki — so much fun!

Ingredients

1 cup cabbage, finely sliced
1 spring onion, finely sliced
½ cup cooked prawns, roughly chopped
1 egg
1 tsp soy sauce
½ cup flour
½ cup water
1 tbsp vegetable oil

To serve

Japanese kewpie mayo
Kecap manis (thick soy sauce)
Sriracha sauce
Crispy shallots
Handful fresh coriander leaves

Makes *1 serve*
Takes *15 minutes*

Dairy-free

Method

Gently mix together cabbage, spring onion, prawns, egg, soy sauce, flour and water in a bowl. Season with salt and freshly ground black pepper.

Heat oil in a frying pan over low to medium heat. Tip the pancake mixture into the pan and use a spoon to spread it evenly around the pan to form a round pancake, approximately 2cm thick. Cook low and slow until it's golden brown on the bottom. Carefully flip and cook the other side until golden. Remember that it is thick and you want it to cook through so the pancake isn't raw in the middle — cover with a lid to help the cooking process if you need to.

Serve with lashings of Japanese mayo, kekap manis and sriracha sauce, a handful of crispy shallots and fresh coriander.

Tip *Swap out prawns for chicken, pork, squid, octopus — any cooked meat really — the beauty of this recipe is to use things up. Or keep them vegetarian and add a Korean twist with a couple of spoonfuls of homemade kimchi,* *see page 17.*

Orange & Chocolate Tiramisu

This is a lighter tiramisu than the traditional version, without custard or coffee, and it reminds me of those chocolate orange balls you get at Christmas-time that break into segments when you tap them. Make ahead, as it tastes even better left to chill overnight and enjoyed the following day.

Ingredients

Chocolate cream
250ml cream
4 tbsp cocoa powder
¼ cup icing sugar

Mascarpone cream
250g mascarpone
¼ cup icing sugar
1 tsp vanilla extract
4 egg whites

Tiramisu
½ cup Grand Marnier
½ cup water
1 orange, zested & juiced
18 savoiardi (ladyfinger) biscuits
8 tbsp orange marmalade
3 tbsp cocoa powder
50g dark chocolate, finely grated

Makes *6 serves*
Takes *20 minutes plus chilling time*

Gluten-free

Method

To make the chocolate cream, place the cream, cocoa powder and icing sugar in a bowl and beat with an electric mixer until soft peaks form. Put to one side.

To make the mascarpone cream, beat together the mascarpone, icing sugar and vanilla in a large bowl. In a separate bowl, whisk the egg whites until stiff peaks form. Add 2 heaped tablespoons of egg whites back into the mascarpone to loosen it, and then fold in the rest of the egg whites so you have a light, frothy cream. Put to one side.

Mix Grand Marnier, water, orange zest and orange juice together in a small bowl. Soak the biscuits one by one for a few seconds, squeezing out any excess liquid and placing on a plate once soaked. Halve the biscuits and place in a single layer in the bottom of six glass tumblers or serving bowls. Spoon some marmalade over the biscuits, followed by a layer of chocolate cream and a layer of mascarpone cream. Repeat the layers until all of the ingredients have been used, ending with the mascarpone. Chill for at least an hour, or overnight.

To serve, dust with cocoa powder and sprinkle with dark chocolate.

Tip *Grand Marnier is an orange-flavoured cognac. You can substitute brandy, rum or Amaretto instead.*

Lemon & Coconut Raw Balls

This is a seemingly simple recipe but the fresh lemon zest and juice really makes these bliss balls POP! When I'm looking for a healthier alternative to that sugar craving, I turn to these tasty little morsels. These balls are delicious made with orange zest and orange juice instead of lemon, too!

Ingredients

1 cup ground almonds
1 ½ cups desiccated coconut, plus extra for rolling
4 tbsp coconut oil
4 tbsp honey
1 large lemon, zested & juiced
1 tsp vanilla extract
1 pinch sea salt

Makes *18 balls*
Takes *10 minutes*

Gluten-free | Dairy-free

Method

Place all of the ingredients into a food processor. Pulse a few times until the mixture starts to hold together.

Roll the mixture into small round balls with your hands. Place the extra desiccated coconut in a shallow bowl and roll the balls until well coated.

Chill in the fridge for 30 minutes before serving.

Tip *If you want to make these bliss balls vegan, omit the honey and use a natural sweetener or some good-quality maple syrup.*

Chocolate Self-Saucing Pudding

I love a good pud in the heart of winter and a self-saucing one? Even better. Ooey, gooey, comforting and delicious. This one is easily made with staple pantry ingredients and is sure to please the whole family! Serve with whipped cream or your favourite vanilla ice cream.

Ingredients

60g butter, melted
½ cup milk
½ tsp vanilla extract
1 egg
1 cup self-raising flour
1 cup caster sugar
½ cup cocoa powder, plus extra for dusting
2 cups boiling water
Vanilla ice cream, to serve

Makes *6 serves*
Takes *40 minutes*

Method

Preheat oven to 160°C.

Grease a 20cm x 20cm ovenproof baking dish.

In a bowl, whisk together the butter, milk, vanilla and egg.

Sift the flour, ½ cup sugar and ¼ cup cocoa powder into a separate bowl. Make a well in the centre and pour wet ingredients into the well, folding together gently.

Spread mixture evenly into the greased dish. Combine the remaining ½ cup sugar and ½ cup cocoa powder and sprinkle over the top of the pudding. Carefully pour boiling water over the top of the pudding.

Bake for 30 minutes, or until the top is firm. Remove from the oven and stand for 10 minutes. Dust the warm pudding with extra cocoa powder and serve immediately with vanilla ice cream.

Tip *You can make this in a round cake tin if you don't have a small enough ovenproof baking dish.*

Heal Meals

Meals that warm you from the inside out like a giant hug — when I'm in need of some nourishment and comfort, I turn to these dishes.

Roasted Carrot & Orange Soup

Roasting carrots brings out their natural sweetness, but even better – it makes this a one-tray soup! Simple, healthy and delicious. Avoid blending the cooked orange slices as the pith makes this soup too bitter, but feel free to play around to get your preferred balance. A knob of ginger is a great flavoursome addition and also helps fight colds in winter, too!

Ingredients

500g carrots, cut into wedges
2 onions, peeled and cut into wedges
1 head garlic, top cut off
2 tsp fennel seeds
1 tsp cumin seeds
2 tbsp olive oil
2 oranges
2 cups vegetable stock

***Makes** 4 serves*
***Takes** 40 minutes*

Gluten-free | Dairy-free | Vegan

Method

Preheat oven to 180°C.

Line a roasting tray with baking paper and add the carrots, onions, garlic, fennel seeds and cumin seeds. Drizzle with olive oil, and gently toss to coat. Slice one of the oranges into rounds and place on top of the carrots. Roast for 25–30 minutes, until the carrots are soft and lightly browned

Zest and juice the remaining orange. Discard the cooked orange slices and squeeze out the cooked garlic, discarding the skins. Add orange zest and juice to a blender along with the garlic, the carrots and all of their juices. Season with salt and freshly ground black pepper. Add half of the vegetable stock and blend, adding more stock as necessary, until you have a smooth soup. Taste, and adjust seasoning if needed.

Serve hot with a drizzle of olive oil and some freshly ground black pepper.

***Tip** Add coconut cream or natural yoghurt before serving to make this soup smooth and creamy.*

Cook's Note

Make it keto-friendly by swapping the kumara mash for cauliflower mash and sprinkling Parmesan over the top before baking.

Paleo Shepherd's Pie

This is one of our frozen meal staples and it's not hard to see why — full of flavour and healthy! With a rich beef filling and a creamy kumara mash, it's comfort food without the grease factor and ticks a variety of allergy boxes, too... it's gluten-free, wheat-free, grain-free, dairy-free, refined sugar-free and soy-free.

Ingredients

2 tbsp coconut oil
2 onions, diced
4 cloves garlic, crushed
600g good-quality beef mince
50g tomato paste
1x 400g can chopped tomatoes
1 cup beef stock
2 tbsp balsamic vinegar
2 tbsp fish sauce
2 tbsp ground cumin
1 tbsp ground coriander
2 tsp ground cinnamon
2 tbsp dried oregano
1 tsp dried chilli flakes
1 tsp smoked paprika
500g kumara, peeled & diced
½ cup coconut cream
2 tbsp pumpkin seeds

Makes *6 serves*
Takes *60 minutes*

Gluten-free | Dairy-free

Method

Preheat oven to 180°C.

Heat the coconut oil in a large, heavy-based saucepan. Add the onion and a pinch of salt and cook for 3–4 minutes until translucent, stirring occasionally. Add the garlic and cook for another 2 minutes.

Push the onion and garlic to one side of the pan and add the mince. Cook, stirring with a wooden spoon to break up the mince, for about 8 minutes or until well browned. Add the tomato paste and cook for another minute. Add the tomatoes, beef stock, balsamic vinegar, fish sauce, cumin, coriander, cinnamon, oregano, chilli flakes and paprika and stir well. Bring to the boil, then reduce heat to low. Simmer, uncovered, for about 20 minutes or until the sauce has thickened. Season with salt and freshly ground black pepper.

Meanwhile, bring a large pot of water to the boil. Add kumara and a tbsp salt and cook for 20 minutes, until tender. Drain and place kumara in a bowl. Add coconut cream and mash until smooth. Season with salt and freshly ground black pepper.

Spoon the beef mixture into an ovenproof dish. Top with kumara mash, smoothing to cover evenly. Sprinkle over pumpkin seeds and bake for 25–30 minutes, until golden brown and bubbling.

Beef Brisket Bibimbap Bowl

Punchy Korean flavours, slow-cooked beef, kimchi and rice noodles... this hearty yet aromatic meal is delicious year-round. It's a great way to use up leftover beef short ribs, see page 159, or my homemade kimchi, see page 17. Also excellent served with rice or egg noodles.

Ingredients

1kg beef brisket
½ cup gochujang (Korean hot pepper paste)
½ cup dark soy sauce
¼ cup brown sugar
1 onion, diced
4 cloves garlic, crushed
2 cups beef stock
200g rice noodles
1 tbsp sesame oil
1 cup kimchi
1 cup bean sprouts
2 spring onions, sliced
Handful fresh coriander leaves
Lime wedges, for serving

Makes *4 serves*
Takes *4 hours*

Dairy-free

Method

Preheat your oven to 160°C.

If your brisket doesn't easily fit into your casserole dish, cut it into smaller chunks. Add brisket, gochujang, soy sauce, brown sugar, onion, garlic and beef stock to the dish — the meat should be just covered in liquid.

Cover with a tight-fitting lid and roast for 3–4 hours until the meat is tender and falls apart easily with a fork. Check the meat every hour — if it starts to look dry, add some extra beef stock or water.

Once cooked, remove the beef and shred it using two forks. Reduce the remaining cooking liquid by half. Add the beef back to the reduced sauce and toss to coat. Season with salt and freshly ground black pepper.

Meanwhile, cook rice noodles according to packet instructions. Toss with sesame oil.

Divide noodles evenly between four bowls. Top with brisket, kimchi, bean sprouts, spring onions and fresh coriander leaves. Serve with lime wedges, for squeezing.

Tip *Turn this into an everyday meal by substituting the slow-cooked beef brisket for beef mince — brown the mince in the pan with onion and garlic and add the spices and half the amount of gochujang paste, sugar and soy sauce. You can also add extra vegetables such as shredded cabbage, cucumber, radish, grated carrot, sautéed mushrooms or sautéed spinach.*

Cook's Note

Pimp your pie with a handful of dried currants or cranberries, and the zest of an orange for some added sweetness and flavour. You can use crumbled feta in place of the yoghurt, too.

Persian Lamb Pie

There is nothing more comforting than a crunchy filo pie — especially when it's filled with spiced lamb and some of my favourite warming flavours... cumin, coriander and cinnamon. I sneak some veggies in to make it more hearty (read: healthy) and served with a green salad this is the perfect Sunday entertainers' lunch or a make-ahead everyday meal.

Ingredients

2 tbsp olive oil
4 cloves garlic, finely diced
2 onions, sliced
2 celery stalks, sliced
500g lamb mince
½ tsp ground turmeric
½ tsp ground cinnamon
1 tsp ground cumin
1 tsp ground coriander
1 tsp smoked paprika
1 cup water
250g cauliflower florets
100g spinach leaves
1 cup natural yoghurt
8 sheets filo pastry
Extra olive oil or melted butter, to brush
1 tsp cumin seeds

Makes *6 serves*
Takes *60 minutes*

Method

Preheat oven to 180°C.

In a large frying pan over medium heat, add the olive oil and then the garlic, onion and celery. Saute for 3–4 minutes until translucent. Push to one side and add the lamb mince. Brown the mince, breaking it up with a wooden spoon as you go. Mix the onions back through the lamb. Add the turmeric, cinnamon, cumin, coriander and paprika and cook for 1–2 minutes longer, until the lamb is well browned.

Add the water to the frying pan and then stir in the cauliflower and spinach leaves. Simmer for 10–15 minutes, until the liquid is evaporated and the cauliflower is cooked through. Season with salt and freshly ground black pepper.

Remove the frying pan from the heat. If your frying pan can go in the oven you can leave the lamb mixture in the pan; otherwise spoon the mixture into an oven-proof dish.

Dot the yoghurt over the lamb mixture.

Remove the filo pastry from the packet and place one sheet on a clean surface. Brush with a little olive oil. Add another sheet of filo pastry on top and brush again, repeating until you have 4 layers of filo. Repeat with the remaining 4 sheets of filo pastry. Place the layered filo on top of the lamb filling, crumpling slightly as you go, so that it fits evenly inside the frying pan, with some lumps and bumps. Brush with a little more olive oil and sprinkle the cumin seeds on top.

Bake in the oven for 40 minutes, until golden brown.

Bring Back the Corned Beef

I know what you're thinking — corned beef lived and died in the 90s, but bear with me... with the addition of herbs and fresh oranges, this old-fashioned cut takes on a new lease of life. It's slow-cooked, super-easy and melts in your mouth. You could easily cook this in a crock pot, too — just set and forget.

Ingredients

800g uncooked corned beef brisket
4 fresh bay leaves
4 sprigs fresh parsley
1 tbsp whole black peppercorns
1 tbsp coriander seeds
1 cinnamon quill
1 tsp dried chilli flakes
1 tbsp yellow mustard seeds
2 onions, skin on & halved
1 whole garlic head, cut in half horizontally
1 orange, zested and halved

Makes *4–6 serves*
Takes *4 hours*

Method

Preheat oven to 160°C.

Rinse corned beef and place in a large casserole dish or heavy pot with a lid that can go into the oven. Add enough water to cover. Add bay leaves, parsley, peppercorns, coriander, cinnamon, chilli flakes, mustard seeds, onions, garlic, orange zest and orange halves. Bring to a simmer over medium heat. Skim off any scum that floats to the surface, secure lid and place casserole dish in the oven.

Bake for 4 hours, or until beef is tender to the touch. Remove from the oven and let beef cool in the cooking liquid.

If you're not going to serve the corned beef straight away, transfer to an airtight container, strain the aromatics from the cooking liquid, and pour over as much of the liquid as you can fit in the container. Cover and place in the fridge until needed.

Tip *Double the recipe and use the leftovers to make a delicious Reuben sandwich,* *see page 117,* *and my corned beef balls,* *see page 113.*

Sunday Roast

This succulent roast beef dish is perfect for a long lunch or weekend dinner. I've chosen a sirloin here because it's a more cost-effective cut of beef, but can still be tender and delicious when cooked right. Plus it's delicious cold in sandwiches the following day.

Ingredients

2 tbsp vegetable oil
1.5kg beef sirloin
1 cup red wine
2 cups beef stock
1 bay leaf
2 thyme sprigs
2 tbsp butter

Makes *6 serves*
Takes *1 hour plus resting time*

Gluten-free

Method

Preheat your oven to 180°C.

Season beef all over with salt and freshly ground black pepper.

In an ovenproof skillet or frying pan, heat the oil over medium to high heat until shimmering and then place beef joint fat-side down in the pan. Sizzle for 2–3 minutes to release some of the fat and then turn, sealing and colouring the beef all over, for about 5 minutes.

Return sirloin to fat-side up in the pan and place in the oven — turning sirloin halfway through its cooking time for an even roast. Allow 10–15 minutes per 500g for medium-rare.

Once roasted, remove the beef from the pan, cover with foil and rest for at least 20 minutes before carving.

Pour any excess fat from the frying pan and return to a medium heat on the stove. Once it begins to sizzle, add the wine and allow to reduce. Add beef stock, bay leaf and thyme and simmer for 8–10 minutes, until thickened slightly. Stir in butter, remove from the heat and strain through a sieve. Serve alongside thick slices of roasted beef sirloin.

Tip *If you prefer a thicker gravy, loosen 1–2 teaspoons of cornflour with a little water and then whisk slowly back into the simmering sauce, until it reaches your desired consistency.*

Rosemary Roast Potatoes

Crisp roasties are an essential side to the Sunday roast, and the trick to an epic roast potato is all in the double-cook. The insides stay fluffy and moist while the outsides are golden brown and craggy. I've kept the seasoning simple here but feel free to dust with your favourite herbs and spices before roasting.

Ingredients

800g potatoes, cut into bite-sized pieces, or left whole if using baby potatoes
4 tbsp vegetable oil
2–3 sprigs fresh rosemary, leaves removed
1 head garlic, halved widthways

Makes *6 serves*
Takes *1 hour*

Method

Preheat your oven to 180°C.

Place potatoes in a large saucepan, cover with water, add a decent handful of salt and boil gently for about 15 minutes, until just tender when pierced with a fork. Drain, spread out on a roasting tray in a single layer and allow to cool.

Drizzle potatoes in olive oil and sprinkle over rosemary, tossing to coat. Smash a few of the larger potatoes to ensure you get some extra crispy bits when they roast. Add garlic to the pan and season generously with salt and freshly ground black pepper.

Roast for 45–50 minutes, turning once or twice. The potatoes should be deep golden and crunchy on the outside and fluffy in the middle.

Cook's Note

Swap out olive oil for duck or goose fat for the ultimate roast potato!

WILLOW
MADE IN AUSTRALIA
12" x 9"

Yorkies

My favourite part of a roast dinner when I was a kid were the Yorkshire puddings. The 'secret' to a perfect yorkie is to heat the oil so the batter begins to cook the moment it hits the pan. Work lightly when you're mixing the batter and quickly when you're pouring it, but be very careful not to burn yourself!

Ingredients

½ cup vegetable oil
3 eggs
1 cup milk
1 cup flour

Makes *6 serves*
Takes *25 minutes*

Method

Preheat your oven to 220°C.

Divide oil evenly between the 12 cups of a muffin tin. Place in the oven to heat the oil.

In a medium bowl, beat together eggs and milk. Stir in flour. Season with salt and freshly ground black pepper.

Carefully remove the hot tin from the oven, and quickly and evenly pour the batter into the muffin cups. Return to the oven and bake, undisturbed, for 20 minutes or until the puddings have puffed up gloriously and are golden brown.

Serve immediately.

Tip *Don't open the oven door! Make your yorkies while the roast beef rests, and you can make a gravy while they're in the oven.*

BREAD BAG
juk.
CHOCOLATE
ALMOND
BUTTER
juk.
juk.

Pear Frangipani Tart

This classic baked tart is perfect for when you want to throw something together quickly, with minimal fuss. I found some pears at the market but you could use apples, stone fruit or even frozen berries to get delicious results. Serve warm with yoghurt for dessert or even breakfast!

Ingredients

5 medium pears
½ cup plain flour
½ cup almond flour
Pinch of salt
¾ tsp baking powder
½ tsp ground cinnamon
½ tsp ground cardamom
2 eggs
¼ cup natural yoghurt
¼ cup olive oil
¼ cup honey, or maple syrup
1 tsp vanilla essence

Makes *1 large pie*
Takes *55 minutes*

Method

Preheat oven to 180°C.

Grease a 20cm round baking dish or skillet pan.

Core the pears. Dice two of the pears finely, and thinly slice the remaining three pears to arrange on the top of the cake.

In a medium bowl, mix together the flour, almond flour, salt, baking powder, cinnamon and cardamom.

In another bowl, beat the eggs and add the yoghurt, olive oil, honey, vanilla essence and diced pears, mixing to combine. Add the wet mixture to the dry mixture and fold together until just mixed. Pour the batter into the pre-greased baking dish. Arrange the sliced pairs over the top of the cake.

Bake for 35–40 minutes, until a skewer inserted into the centre of the cake comes out clean. Remove from the oven and cool for 10–15 minutes. Dust with icing sugar just before serving.

Curry Night

Fragrant and aromatic, a spread of warming curries and condiments is one of my go-to entertaining hacks... prepare everything in advance and let your guests help themselves!

Fresh Green Chutney

This thin and zesty green chutney is delicious spooned over just about anything, even eggs! My favourite thing about Indian cuisine is all of the amazing condiments — sweet, salty and sour — and I like to have a little bit of everything on my plate to mop up with a freshly grilled flatbread.

Ingredients

100ml plain yoghurt
1 garlic clove, finely chopped
1 small green chilli, seeds removed and finely chopped
½ cup mint leaves
½ cup coriander leaves
1 tbsp lemon juice

Makes *6 serves*
Takes *5 minutes, plus 30 minutes draining time*

Method

Line a sieve with paper towels, place it over a bowl and pour in the yoghurt. Drain for 30 minutes until the yoghurt is no longer runny. Discard the yoghurt whey and then place the thickened yoghurt into the bowl.

Place the remaining ingredients plus 2 tablespoons of the yoghurt into a blender and blend until you have a smooth paste. Stir into the remaining yoghurt. Season with salt and freshly ground pepper to taste.

Tip *If you're using a naturally thick Greek yoghurt, you can omit the first draining step. Or use a little bit of labneh from my recipe on page 44.*

Tomato Kachumber

Ingredients

250g cherry tomatoes, halved
1 small brown onion, sliced thinly
1 tbsp lemon juice
Pinch cayenne pepper
¼ tsp salt
½ tsp garam masala
Handful fresh mint leaves
Fresh green chilli, sliced
Lemon or lime wedges

Makes *6 serves*
Takes *5 minutes*

Gluten-free | Dairy-free | Vegan

Method

A simple chopped tomato and onion salad is the perfect accompaniment for an Indian banquet – tangy and refreshing. Serve with fresh mint leaves and some wedges of lemon or lime, for squeezing. Gently mix tomatoes, onion, lemon juice, cayenne pepper and salt together in a bowl. Sprinkle over garam masala.

Scatter fresh mint, chilli and lemon or lime wedges, if you like, just before serving.

Tip Make your own garam masala by mixing together 1 tbsp ground cumin, 2 tsp ground coriander, 2 tsp ground cardamom, 1 tsp ground cinnamon, 1 tsp ground black pepper, ½ tsp ground nutmeg, ½ tsp ground cloves and ½ tsp cayenne pepper. To bump up flavour and fragrance, lightly toast the garam masala in a dry pan over medium heat. Store in an airtight jar and use as required.

Cucumber Raita

Ingredients

½ cucumber
1 cup natural yoghurt
1 tsp dried mint
½ lemon, zested & juiced

Makes *6 serves*
Takes *5 minutes*

Gluten-free

Method

The most quintessential of Indian condiments – a mouth-cooling yoghurt dip with grated cucumber to help calm any "irresponsible chilli levels", something I'm prone to doing more often than not!

Grate the cucumber into a bowl, and gently squeeze to remove some of the liquid. Add the remaining ingredients and season to taste with salt and freshly ground black pepper.

Tamarind & Coconut Fish Curry

Fresh and fragrant, this is a soulful curry that's just as enjoyable after a long day at the beach in summer as it is in the heart of winter. Choose a firmer-fleshed fish so it holds up in the sauce and experiment with different types of sustainably-sourced fish — I like it with monkfish or trevally, as well as the more common terakihi, hapuka and gurnard.

Ingredients

2 tbsp coconut oil
4 whole dried chillies
1 tbsp brown mustard seeds
1 tsp coriander seeds
1 tsp cumin seeds
2 sprigs fresh curry leaves, or 1 tsp curry powder
1 onion, sliced
4 garlic cloves, crushed
1 tbsp turmeric
1 tbsp tomato paste
1 tbsp fish sauce
1x 400ml can coconut milk
1x 400ml can diced tomatoes
2 tbsp tamarind puree
600g skinless fish fillets, diced
Large handful coriander
Lemon wedges, to serve

Makes *6 serves*
Takes *20 minutes*

Method

Heat coconut oil in a large, heavy-bottomed saucepan over medium heat. Add chillies, mustard seeds, coriander seeds and cumin seeds and cook for 1–2 minutes, until fragrant and starting to pop. Add curry leaves, onion and garlic and cook, stirring occasionally for 4–5 minutes or until the onions are soft.

Add turmeric and tomato paste and cook for 2 more minutes. Stir in fish sauce, coconut milk, tomatoes and tamarind puree and cook for 5 minutes, until sauce has thickened slightly. Add fish and simmer for 5 minutes or until the fish is just cooked through. Taste and season with salt and freshly ground black pepper.

Serve with coriander leaves and fresh lemon wedges.

Tip *This curry sauce is a great base for chicken too, or keep it vege with chunks of roasted cauliflower and chickpeas (omit the fish sauce).*

Wency's Dhal

A good dhal is like a big hug — warming, comforting and simple yet so deeply complex. While curry powder is a great staple spice to have on hand, the flavours of this delicious dhal are two-fold — firstly, the tempered fresh curry leaves which impart so much richness, and secondly the pinch of asafoetida (sometimes known as hing), the secret dried gum that is a staple in Indian cooking.

Ingredients

4 tbsp vegetable oil
1 onion, thinly sliced
4 cloves garlic, crushed
1 thumb-sized piece of ginger, peeled & grated
1 fresh chilli, deseeded & finely chopped (optional)
1 tsp turmeric
1 pinch asafoetida
2 cups red lentils, washed & drained
1 large tomato, diced
2 stems curry leaves
1 tsp cumin seeds
1 tsp black mustard seeds
1 handful coriander leaves

Makes *6 serves*
Takes *30 minutes*

Gluten-free | Dairy-free | Vegan

Method

In a medium saucepan over medium heat, add 2 tablespoons of oil and sliced onion, sautéing for 1–2 minutes until starting to soften. Add garlic, ginger and chilli (if using) and fry for 1–2 more minutes.

Add tomato, turmeric and asafoetida, stirring well to combine. Add lentils and 4 cups of water, reduce heat to low and simmer for 20 minutes, or until the lentils are cooked.

In a small frying pan over medium heat, add 2 tablespoons of oil and the curry leaves, cumin seeds and mustard seeds. Toast until fragrant, 1–2 minutes. Remove from the heat and pour oil and aromatics straight into the lentils. Season to taste with salt and pepper.

Serve with fresh coriander leaves. You can enjoy your dhal by itself or accompanied by basmati rice, quinoa, roti or naan bread.

Tip *Look for asafoetida in powdered form at an Indian food store. If you're gluten-free, double check it doesn't contain wheat flour.*

Vegan Chickpea Curry

Chickpeas can take on so much flavour, and hold their texture wonderfully. I keep this sauce thick so you can smoosh it onto flatbreads or enjoy it as a side dish with other curries. Add as much chilli as you and your family enjoy. It's great spread cold in wraps and sandwiches the next day, too!

Ingredients

2 tbsp vegetable oil
1 tbsp brown mustard seeds
1 tsp coriander seeds
1 tsp cumin seeds
2 sprigs fresh curry leaves, or 1 tsp curry powder
1 onion, thinly sliced
4 cloves garlic, crushed
1 thumb-sized piece of ginger, peeled & grated
1 fresh chilli, deseeded & finely chopped (optional)
1 tbsp tomato paste
1 tbsp garam masala, *see page 201*
1x 400ml can diced tomatoes, drained
1x 400ml can chickpeas, drained
½ cup coconut cream
1 lemon, juiced
Large handful coriander

Makes *6 serves*
Takes *20 minutes*

Gluten-free | Dairy-free | Vegan

Method

Heat oil in a large, heavy-bottomed saucepan over medium heat. Add mustard seeds, coriander seeds and cumin seeds and cook for 1-2 minutes, until fragrant and starting to pop. Add curry leaves, onion, garlic and ginger and cook, stirring occasionally for 4-5 minutes or until the onions are soft.

Add tomato paste and garam masala and cook for 2 more minutes. Stir in diced tomatoes, chickpeas and coconut cream and simmer for 5 minutes, until sauce is thick. Add lemon juice to taste and season with salt and freshly ground black pepper.

Serve with fresh coriander leaves.

Tip *Fry off some extra curry leaves in a little vegetable oil to add as a garnish for extra flavour and crunch.*

Amit's Flatbreads

I generally have a pack or two of store-bought Indian breads in the freezer, but when I have the time and inclination to make these breads from scratch, I always vow to never use the packet breads again! So light and pillowy, and perfect for scooping up the last of the curry sauce. This is one of my chef's yeast-free recipes, which I now swear by.

Ingredients

2 ½ cups plain flour
½ tsp baking powder
¼ tsp baking soda
½ cup natural yoghurt
1 tsp salt
2 tsp white sugar
1 tsp cumin seeds
2 tbsp canola oil, plus extra for frying

Makes *6 serves*
Takes *1 ½ hours*

Method

Place flour, baking powder and baking soda in a bowl and mix well to combine. Pass through a sieve.

In another bowl, mix together yoghurt, salt and sugar. Fold through the cumin seeds.

Add the wet mixture to the flour mixture and combine gradually to form a dough, adding up to a cup of water to bring it together. Lightly knead until the mixture is soft and pillowy.

Incorporate 2 tablespoons of oil into the dough and cover dough with a damp cloth. Sit to one side for an hour.

Divide the dough into 16 equal portions. Roll them into balls. Place on a tray, cover again with a damp cloth and let them rest for 10–15 minutes.

Grease your palms with a little oil and flatten the balls. Roll out into 12cm disks.

Fill a large pot or saucepan with enough oil for shallow frying and bring up to a medium-high temperature. Add the breads to the oil one or two at a time and fry on both sides until lightly browned. Remove and drain on absorbent paper. Keep wrapped and warm in a clean tea towel until all of the breads have been fried off and serve immediately.

Tip *You can leave out the cumin seeds for plain flatbreads, or experiment with different flavours. For garlic flatbreads, combine some finely diced garlic with butter and brush over the flatbreads when they're hot out of the frying pan.*

Backyard BBQ

Summertime spells cocktails, alfresco dining and cooking over coals — expand your backyard repertoire with these entertaining eats.

weber

Nacho Popcorn

Step up your popcorn game — home-popped kernels are a cheap and easy snack, plus you can control exactly what ingredients you use... make them as healthy or as buttery as you like! Serve these up for pre-dinner snacking at your next barbecue or get-together as a nice change from chips & dip.

Ingredients

1 tbsp vegetable oil
½ cup popcorn kernels
1 tsp salt
1 tsp fennel seeds
½ tsp ground cumin
½ tsp smoked paprika
½ tsp dried chilli flakes
¼ tsp cayenne pepper
2 tbsp salted butter, melted
½ cup finely grated Parmesan

Makes *8 cups*
Takes *10 minutes*

Gluten-free

Method

In a large, covered saucepan over medium heat, add oil and popcorn kernels. Heat until the popping stops, shaking gently. Remove from heat.

In a small bowl or jar, mix together salt, fennel seeds, cumin, smoked paprika, chilli flakes and cayenne pepper.

Pour butter and taco seasoning over popcorn, replace lid and shake pot until the popcorn is well covered.

Taste and season with salt, if needed. Sprinkle over Parmesan cheese just before serving.

Tip *You can use store-bought taco seasoning to whip this up in a hurry!*

Easy Oven Baked Chips with Chicken Salt

I keep these chips oven-baked to balance out the naughtiness of the chicken salt I smother them in, because if you know me well, it's no secret that I have a soft spot for fried chicken. And, ahem... the secret herbs and spices that go on those golden fries. Avoid a crowded tray to make sure the chips are crispy on the outside and soft and tender on the inside. You can easily make kumara wedges with this recipe, too.

Ingredients

Chicken salt

200g chicken skin
6 tbsp salt
3 tbsp garlic powder
3 tbsp sweet paprika
1 tsp ground white pepper
1 tsp onion powder

Chips

6 large roasting potatoes, cut lengthways into wedges
¼ cup plain flour
¼ cup olive oil
2 tbsp chicken salt

Makes *6 serves*
Takes *30 minutes*

Dairy-free

Method

Preheat oven to 180°C.

To make the chicken salt, trim meat and excess fat from chicken skin and cut into 10cm pieces. Flatten, flesh-side down, on a lined baking tray. Season with salt and pepper and top with another layer of baking paper and another baking tray. Bake until golden brown and crispy, about 1 hour. Allow to cool for 10 minutes.

Place chicken skins into a food processor along with salt, garlic powder, paprika, pepper and onion powder. Blitz to a fine powder.

To make the chips, place potato wedges in a bag and add the flour. Seal and shake until the wedges are finely coated. Place on a lined baking tray, drizzle with olive oil and bake, turning once, until golden and cooked through — around 25 minutes.

Season with chicken salt and serve immediately.

Tip *DIY poutine with a quick and easy gravy recipe — heat 1 tbsp oil over medium heat then add ½ finely sliced onion and gently saute until slightly caramelized. Stir in 1 tbsp flour and 2 cups beef stock and cook gently over low heat until thickened. Season with 1 tbsp malt vinegar and 1 tbsp Worcestershire sauce, plus salt and freshly ground black pepper. Serve chips with a drizzle of hot gravy, a few blobs of sour cream and some finely grated Parmesan to finish.*

Cook's Note

Store chicken salt in an airtight container and sprinkle on everything from potatoes to popcorn to the rim of your Bloody Mary.

Grilled Haloumi & Pineapple Skewers

Whether you're vegetarian or not, these meat-free skewers are bursting with flavour and make for a fun barbecue appetiser. Double the dukkah recipe and store in an airtight jar for sprinkling on salads or dipping with olive oil and some wedges of fresh bread.

Ingredients

½ pineapple, peeled, cored and cut into thick wedges
300g haloumi, cut into cubes
½ cup cherry tomatoes
2 tbsp honey
1 tbsp olive oil
1 lemon, zested and juiced
Small handful fresh mint, to serve

Dukkah

1 tbsp cumin seeds, toasted
1 tbsp coriander seeds, toasted
1 tsp whole black peppercorns
1 cup hazelnuts, toasted and skins removed
½ cup sesame seeds, toasted
1 tsp salt

Makes *4 serves*
Takes *15 minutes*

Method

Preheat your barbecue to high.

Thread the pineapple, haloumi and cherry tomatoes onto skewers. Cook for 5-6 minutes, turning occasionally, until the haloumi has charred slightly but isn't too soft.

To make the dukkah, place the cumin, coriander and peppercorns in the bowl of a small food processor and grind until fine (you can also use a mortar & pestle to do this by hand). Add the hazelnuts and sesame seeds and pulse until roughly chopped. Transfer to a bowl and add salt, stirring to combine.

Transfer the skewers onto a serving plate. Drizzle with honey, olive oil and lemon juice. Sprinkle over lemon zest, dukkah and fresh mint to serve.

Tip *I used rosemary twigs (stripped of their leaves) as skewers, for extra flavour and fun. If you're using wooden skewers, soak them for an hour in cold water before using to stop them burning on the barbecue.*

Slow Chicken

Cooking a chicken whole is the cheapest (and often easiest) way to prepare the bird. And since bones help develop great flavour, you're also ending up with a better-tasting meal than if you were eating boneless chicken breasts or thighs. Take your oven outside this summer and tame your bird on the open flame — the trick is to use indirect heat so she cooks evenly and stays juicy.

Ingredients

3 tbsp olive oil
2 tbsp chipotle sauce
2 garlic cloves, crushed
1 lemon, zested & juiced
2 tsp honey
2 tsp smoked paprika
1 tsp ground cumin
1 tsp ground coriander
½ tsp ground cinnamon
1 tsp salt
1 whole brined chicken, about 1.6kg (see page 236 for brining techniques)

Makes *4 serves*
Takes *2 hours*

Method

Mix together olive oil, chipotle sauce, garlic, lemon zest and juice, honey, paprika, cumin, coriander, oregano and salt in a small bowl. Rub all over the chicken, rubbing some under the skin of the breast and thighs. Let the chicken sit at room temperature, covered, for 30 minutes.

Prepare your barbecue: for gas grills, turn all of the burners on to medium-high, and then after 15 minutes turn the middle burner off and the remaining burners down to low. For charcoal grills: light charcoal on one side of the drip pan and let it burn until the coals are glowing red and coated in grey ash, about 15 minutes.

Place the chicken breast-side up over the middle burner or on the indirect side of the grill, cover and cook for about 75 minutes, until the leg juices run clear or the internal temperature reads 75°C. If you're using charcoal, you may need to add extra coals during cooking). All barbecues are different, and you know yours best so adjust the cooking time to suit.

Remove chicken from the barbecue and rest for at least 15 minutes before carving.

Cook's Note

For the ultimate in slow, you can cook this whole chicken in the slow cooker all year round! Place the marinated chicken in your crock pot, add and cook for 8 hours on low or 4 hours on high. Place under the grill for 10 minutes to brown, before serving.

Wedge Salad Favourites

Bring back the iceberg, I say! Sometimes a simple crunchy side is all you need, especially in the throws of summer. Here are my best-dressed wedges, ready for barbecue season.

Blue cheese dressing

Mash 150g blue cheese with a fork and stir in ½ cup crème fraiche or sour cream. Add 1 tbsp chopped chives, a squeeze of lemon juice and just enough milk to give your dressing a drizzle-worthy consistency. Season with salt and freshly ground black pepper.

Sundried tomato dressing

Finely chop ¼ cup of sundried tomatoes and ½ a small red onion. Whisk together with 1 tsp honey, 3 tbsp of red wine vinegar, 1 tbsp of oil from the sundried tomato jar and an extra 2 tbsp of olive oil. Season with salt and freshly ground black pepper. Add ½ tsp dried chilli flakes if you like a kick.

Tahini dressing

Whisk together 2 tbsp tahini, the juice of half a lemon, 2 tbsp olive oil, 1 small crushed garlic clove, ½ tsp ground cumin and a pinch of cayenne pepper. Add 2–3 tbsp ice-cold water until you reach your desired consistency — it might look broken at first but it'll come together into a creamy emulsion as you whisk. Season with salt and freshly ground black pepper.

Rocket & caper dressing

In a small food processor, blend 2 tbsp capers, 3 anchovy fillets, a large handful of rocket leaves and the juice of a small lemon. Drizzle in 4 good glugs of olive oil while blending, until you have a loose sauce. Season with salt and freshly ground black pepper.

Japanese sesame dressing

Whisk together 2 tbsp tahini, 50ml rice wine vinegar, 2 tsp soy sauce, 1 small crushed garlic clove, a few drops of sesame oil and 1 tsp mirin. Add 2–3 tbsp water to give your dressing a drizzle-worthy consistency. Season with salt and freshly ground black pepper. Sprinkle over toasted sesame seeds to serve.

Ranch-style dressing

Whisk or shake together in a jar 2/3 cup buttermilk, 2 tbsp mayonnaise, 2 tbsp sour cream, 1 small crushed garlic clove, 1 tsp Dijon mustard and 2 tbsp of finely chopped fresh herbs — dill, parsley, basil, chives or tarragon all work well. Add a pinch of cayenne pepper, a pinch of smoked paprika and season with salt and freshly ground black pepper.

Fast Slaw

This is my go-to, throw-together summer slaw, hence the name. It's easy, creamy and fresh, and perfect for serving alongside grilled meats and veggies at your next barbecue. Use a food processor with a slicer attachment for extra-quick prep, and add any extra ingredients you have on hand to put your own spin on it.

Ingredients

½ red cabbage
½ green cabbage
1 red onion
3 carrots
Large handful parsley, roughly chopped
1 cup mayonnaise
2 tbsp apple cider vinegar
2 tbsp Dijon mustard
1 tsp sugar
1 tsp celery seeds or celery salt

Makes *6–8 serves*
Takes *10 minutes*

Method

Quarter the cabbages, cut out the core and slice into thin shreds — you can use a knife, a mandoline, or a food processor with a slicing attachment.

Thinly slice the red onion — again, using a knife, a mandolin or a food processor with a slicing attachment.

Peel and grate or shred the carrots — using a grater, a mandolin or a food processor with a julienne attachment.

In a large bowl toss together cabbage, red onion, carrot and parsley.

In a smaller bowl, stir together the mayonnaise, vinegar, mustard, sugar and celery seeds, and season with salt and freshly ground black pepper.

Pour half of the dressing over the slaw and mix well with your hands. Add more dressing it seems a little dry.

Cook's Note

Apple cider vinegar adds zest and freshness to the dressing, but you can substitute for whatever vinegar you have on hand, like red wine vinegar or white wine vinegar.

Festive Feast

A Kiwi Christmas feast is about big, vibrant flavours, the best seasonal produce and delicious meats (finished on the barbie, if you wish) that are sure to impress.

Citrus Couscous with Orange Paprika Vinaigrette

A fresh and zesty citrus salad that packs a sweet punch. Keep an eye out for interesting varieties of oranges like blood oranges or red navel oranges; grapefruit is a wonderful addition to this salad, too. You can substitute Israeli pearl couscous or quinoa as the base grain of this salad.

Ingredients

2 cups chicken or vegetable stock
2 cups Moroccan couscous
¼ cup dried apricots, roughly chopped
1 tbsp olive oil
2 oranges, zested and peeled
Handful fresh mint leaves

Orange paprika vinaigrette

1 tsp Dijon mustard
1 tsp honey
½ tsp smoked paprika
2 tbsp red wine vinegar
½ cup olive oil

***Makes** 4–6 serves as a side dish*
***Takes** 15 minutes*

Dairy-free

Method

Bring the stock to the boil in a medium-sized saucepan. When the stock is boiling, remove from the heat, add the couscous, half the orange zest, dried apricot and olive oil. Cover and leave for 5 minutes, until all of the stock has been absorbed. Fluff the couscous mixture with a fork. Allow to cool.

Portion the oranges into segments, over a small bowl to catch any juice, and place to one side. To the orange juice, add the remaining orange zest, Dijon mustard, honey, paprika, red wine vinegar and olive oil and whisk well to combine. Season with salt and freshly ground black pepper.

Just before serving toss the oranges through the couscous along with a generous drizzle of the orange paprika vinaigrette, and top with fresh mint leaves.

Cook's Note

Turn this into an easy everyday meal and serve with grilled chicken or fish, plus an extra drizzle of the smoky orange paprika vinaigrette.

Zucchini Ribbon Salad with Pomegranate

This is a simple salad but sometimes the simplest things in life are the most pleasing! The pops of pomegranate add a festive touch and it's the perfect side for barebecued meats. Make a big batch of the green dressing to keep in the fridge for throwing together easy salads over the holiday period, or serving with barbecued meat.

Ingredients

2–3 zucchini
100g feta
½ pomegranate, deseeded
Large handful parsley leaves

Green dressing

1 garlic clove
1 tsp Dijon mustard
3 tsp lemon juice
1 tsp sugar
½ tsp chilli flakes
Large handful parsley, including stems
Large handful coriander, including roots
Large handful spinach
1 tsp white wine vinegar
½ cup rice bran oil

Makes *4–6 serves as a side dish*
Takes *10 minutes*

Gluten-free

Method

Using a vegetable peeler, ribbon lengths of zucchini into a bowl. Toss together with feta, pomegranate and parsley.

To make the green dressing, add the garlic, mustard, lemon juice, sugar and chilli flakes to the bowl of your food processor. Pulse to break down the garlic. Add the herbs and spinach, then blitz to a paste. With the food processor still running, add the vinegar and then drizzle in the oil. Season with salt and freshly cracked black pepper to taste.

Drizzle the salad with a generous amount of green dressing just before serving.

Tip *Ribbon the zucchini in advance and store them covered in water in the fridge. They'll stay crisp — just drain well before serving.*

Brining Chicken

While it might seem like a faff, brining your chicken before cooking will seriously increase the seasoning, tenderness and juiciness of your bird, especially when cooked on the bone. The process of osmosis helps the chicken to absorb water (and inadvertently, a wonderful savoury flavour through salt and seasoning), keeping more natural moisture within the bird as it cooks.

Ingredients

Small handful fresh thyme leaves
1 lemon, halved
2 tbsp black peppercorns
½ cup salt
½ cup brown sugar
1 cup apple cider vinegar
3 litres water

***Makes** 3 litres brining liquid*
***Takes** 10 minutes, plus overnight*

Gluten-free | Dairy-free

Method

Place all of the ingredients in a large saucepan over high heat, and bring to the boil. Cook for 3–4 minutes, until the salt and sugar have completely dissolved. Remove pan from the heat and allow to cool completely (add some ice to help speed up this process, if you're short on time).

Place chicken in the brine, cover and refrigerate for 4–8 hours, or overnight.

To cook, remove the chicken from the brine, rinse under cold water and pat dry with paper towels before cooking.

***Tip** You can use this simple brine on chicken pieces and even boneless thigh and breast, just don't brine for quite so long or your chicken will be overly salty. Try 1 hour for boneless chicken and 1–2 hours for bone-in thighs or legs. You can brine pork chops or loin roasts, too.*

Experiment with different flavours in your brining liquid — fresh or dried herbs and spices, aromatics like onions, garlic, ginger and fennel, or even add sweetness by adding maple syrup or fruit juices.

99% PURE
STRONG-LITE

A Zillion Herbs Butterflied Chicken

The key to this recipe is turning whatever herbs you have on hand into a delicious, fresh marinade that'll colour your chicken wonderfully. Spatchcocking your chicken will make it cook faster and also allow for more of those gorgeous charred bits of skin that epitomise summer barbecue cooking over the holiday period.

Ingredients

1 whole chicken

Green sauce

6 garlic cloves, peeled
1 red onion, peeled & quartered
1 handful coriander, leaves and stems
1 handful basil, leaves and stems
1 handful mint, thicker stems removed
1 handful parsley, leaves and stems
1 handful spinach leaves
1 tbsp Dijon mustard
4 tbsp fish sauce
2 tbsp honey
1 lemon, zested & juiced
2 tbsp olive oil

Makes *4 serves*
Takes *45 minutes plus marinating time*

Gluten-free | Dairy-free

Method

To spatchcock your chicken, place the chicken breast-side down with the legs facing you. Cut along each side of the backbone. Open the chicken out and turn it over to flatten the breastbone by pressing down with the heel of your hand.

Add all of the green sauce ingredients to a blender or food processor and blitz into a smooth sauce. Taste and season with salt and freshly ground black pepper.

Place the chicken in a large bowl, or in a large ziplock bag, and pour the green sauce over. Make sure the chicken is well coated, place in the fridge and marinate for at least an hour, or overnight.

Preheat a lidded barbecue to 180°C. Place chicken, breast-side up on the hot plate, close the lid and cook for around 20 minutes. Flip the chicken over and place it skin-side down on the hotter side of the grill and cook for a further 15–20 minutes, until crispy-skinned and cooked through.

Chicken should have an internal temperature of 75°C. Rest before carving and serving.

Tip *If you're cooking in an oven, place chicken breast-side up in an ovenproof dish and roast at 180°C for 40 minutes, or until golden brown and cooked through.*

When daylight savings is in full swing, there's no reason you can't throw this on the grill for an easy everyday meal, too!

Lemon & Sage Roasted Turkey

Turkey was never a Christmas ritual for me growing up, but I've come to appreciate the sentiment and tradition it holds. Turkey isn't a common protein in New Zealand (yet) so I like the habit of enjoying it once a year, at Christmas. Source a good quality, free-range bird if possible — there are a couple of family-run businesses in the South Island who are truly passionate about what they do.

Ingredients

4kg turkey
250g butter, at room temperature, plus extra melted butter for basting
¼ cup sage leaves, finely chopped, plus large handful of extra leaves for stuffing
2 tbsp freshly grated lemon zest
1 tsp smoked paprika
2–3 whole lemons

Makes *6–8 serves*
Takes *3+ hours*

Method

On Christmas Eve — Remove the neck and giblets, and pat the turkey dry all over. In a small bowl mash together butter, sage, lemon zest, paprika and a generous pinch of salt and pepper.

Starting at the neck end of the turkey, loosen the skin of the breast by gently sliding your fingers underneath. Rub half of the flavoured butter under the skin. Loosen skin around the legs and the thighs and rub the remaining flavoured butter under the skin. Season the turkey inside and out with a generous amount of salt and freshly ground black pepper. Stuff the cavity with lemons and extra sage. Place the turkey, breast side down, in a large, lined roasting tray and refrigerate, uncovered, overnight.

On Christmas Day — Bring turkey to room temperature 45 minutes before you want to start cooking. Preheat your oven to 230°C.

Flip the turkey breast-side up and add 2 cups of water to the bottom of the tray. Cover with foil. Place tray in the bottom half of your oven and immediately turn the temperature down to 180°C. Roast for 2½ hours, basting turkey every 20 minutes with juices from the bottom of the pan and extra melted butter, if needed.

Remove foil and roast for another 30–45 minutes, until golden brown and leg juices are running clear. Rest for at least 45 minutes before carving.

Cook's Note

This recipe is simple and fool-proof; if your turkey is smaller or larger then just make sure you adjust the cooking time accordingly!

Negroni-Glazed Ham

Ham is the star of the show on Christmas Day, and a large leg of ham will keep you happily fed for at least a week post-Christmas. You can serve it hot, straight out of the oven, or glaze your ham a day or two in advance to leave oven space for other dishes.

Ingredients

2 cups Negroni marmalade, see page 65, or orange marmalade
1 thumb fresh ginger, peeled and grated
2 cloves garlic, crushed
4 star anise
2 cups brown sugar
2 tbsp seeded mustard, plus extra for serving
1 whole ham on the bone, cooked

Makes 12 serves
Takes 1 ½ hours

Method

Preheat oven to 180°C.

Place a medium saucepan over medium heat, and add the marmalade, ginger, garlic, star anise, brown sugar, mustard and 3 cups of water. Bring to a gentle simmer and cook for 10–15 minutes, until sticky and slightly reduced. Remove from the heat. Season with salt and freshly ground black pepper.

Carefully remove the skin from your ham (the easiest way to do this is by running your fingers gently under the skin) so you're left with a nice layer of fat. Score the fat with a knife, and brush with half the glaze.

Place ham on a greased wire rack sitting inside a large roasting tray. Pour two cups of water around the base of the ham. Cook for up to an hour on the bottom shelf of your oven, brushing with extra glaze every 15 minutes, until golden brown and sticky.

Serve ham with remaining glaze and extra seeded mustard.

Tip *To stop your leftover ham from drying out, keep it in a ham-bag, old pillowcase or wrap it in a clean tea-towel in the fridge. Before using the bag, soak in a mix of 1 litre of water and 2 tbsp white vinegar. Wring out the excess liquid to leave the bag damp. Repeat every few days and your bone-in ham will last for up to two weeks.*

Jamaican Jerk Salmon with Tropical Salsa

This summery salmon dish will be the hero of your Christmas spread with its mouthwatering marinade and fresh tropical salsa. You can spice up or tone down the jerk to suit the crowd – and add it to your repertoire for marinating chicken, pork or even haloumi steaks! Keep it gluten-free by using gluten-free tamari instead of regular soy sauce.

Ingredients

1 whole salmon fillet, skin-on and pin-boned, roughly 1.5kg

Jerk marinade

2–3 spring onions
1 small red onion
3 garlic cloves, smashed
3 tbsp soy sauce
1 tbsp lime juice
1 tbsp cider vinegar
1 tbsp fresh thyme leaves
2 tbsp brown sugar
1 tsp smoked paprika
1 tsp ground allspice
1 tsp dried chilli flakes
½ tsp ground nutmeg
½ tsp ground cinnamon
3 tbsp vegetable oil

Tropical salsa

½ fresh pineapple, cored & diced
1 small red onion, diced
1 zucchini, diced
Handful coriander, finely chopped
1 lime, zested & juiced
1 small fresh red chilli, deseeded & finely chopped

Makes *8–10 serves*
Takes *30 minutes*

Dairy-free

Method

Preheat oven to 180°C.

To make the jerk marinade, place all of the ingredients in a blender and blitz to a smooth paste. Taste and adjust if needed.

Place salmon fillet skin-down on a lined baking tray. Check for bones; remove with kitchen tweezers if you find any. Rub all over with jerk marinade. Place in the oven and bake for 20–22 minutes, until just cooked through and still tender to the touch.

Meanwhile, make the tropical salsa. Combine all of the ingredients in a medium bowl, tossing to coat.

Place the salmon on a serving dish and scatter half of the tropical salsa over the top, serving the rest in a bowl on the side, along with fresh lime wedges.

Tip *To babecue your salmon, preheat a lidded babecue to 200°C. Place salmon (skin down) on the hot plate, close the lid and cook for 13–15 minutes, until just cooked through and still tender to the touch. Remove carefully with a long fish slice before serving with the tropical salsa.*

Dukkah-Rubbed Christmas Lamb

Is there anything more quintessentially Kiwi on Christmas Day than a roast lamb? The traditional leg gets a modern refresh with a Middle Eastern-inspired almond dukkah rub — baste when you remember for maximum tenderness. This is great to have in the fridge for Boxing Day leftovers, too!

Ingredients

¼ cup whole almonds
3 tbsp coriander seeds
3 tbsp cumin seeds
3 tbsp sesame seeds
1 tsp fennel seeds
1 tsp dried mint
1 whole leg of lamb, approximately 1.6–1.8kg
3 tbsp olive oil

***Makes** 6–8 serves as a main dish*
***Takes** 1 ½ hours*

Gluten-free | Dairy-free

Method

Preheat oven to 180°C.

In a food processor, combine almonds, coriander, cumin, sesame, fennel and mint. Pulse until a coarse spice mix forms. Season with salt and freshly ground black pepper.

Pat lamb dry, drizzle with olive oil and dress with the dukkah rub, pushing it onto the lamb as you go. Place in a roasting tray and bake for 1¼ hours for medium, or 1½–2 hours for well done. Baste with juices 2–3 times during cooking. Remove the lamb from the oven, cover and allow to rest for at least 20 minutes before serving.

***Tip** To barbecue your lamb, preheat a lidded barbecue to 200°C. Place lamb in the centre of the barbecue and turn the burners directly under the lamb off, so just the side burners are going. Close the lid and cook for 2½–3 hours, until cooked to your liking. Remember to rest your lamb before serving, as above.*

Mustard-Rolled Eye Fillet with Rosemary Salt

A tender cut of beef like this is pure luxury on the Christmas table — simple but so delicious. After roasting, cover the meat with foil and rest for at least 10 minutes to allow the meat to relax. Up the ante and serve with our easy homemade rosemary salt.

Ingredients

Eye fillet

1.5kg whole eye fillet steak
3 tbsp Dijon mustard
3 tbsp seeded mustard
1 tbsp balsamic vinegar
½ cup olive oil
3 cloves garlic, crushed

Salt

½ cup table salt
2–3 sprigs fresh rosemary, leaves picked
1 cup flaky sea salt

Makes *8–10 serves*
Takes *30 minutes*

Method

For the eye fillet — Preheat oven to 200°C.

In a small bowl, whisk together both mustards, balsamic vinegar, oil and garlic.

Trim silverskin off the beef if necessary. Season generously all over with salt and freshly cracked black pepper.

Heat a large nonstick frying pan over high heat and seal the beef on each side for 1–2 minutes, until brown.

Remove beef from the pan, brush with mustard mixture and place in a lined ovenproof dish (if your frying pan is oven-safe, you can reuse this). Roast for 20–23 minutes for medium rare, or until cooked to your liking.

Cover with foil and rest for 10–15 minutes before carving.

For the salt — Preheat oven to 100°C.

Place the table salt and rosemary in a small food processor and pulse until combined. Mix through the flaky sea salt.

Spread salt mixture out on a baking tray and bake for 1 hour, stirring occasionally, until dried out.

Store in an airtight container for up to 4 weeks.

Cook's Note

Ask your butcher for a middle-cut piece of fillet so the beef is the same thickness throughout to cook evenly.

Leftover Turkey Ramen

While soup isn't something we necessarily turn to in the summer months, this is fresh and cleansing and a different way to use up leftover turkey from Christmas dinner. Save the pan juices from your turkey roast, plus the bones, to create a delightfully rich yet light umami-laced broth.

Ingredients

Reserved turkey carcass and/or bones
2 bunches spring onions
1 thumb-size piece of ginger, peeled & grated
1 head garlic, halved crosswise
2 tbsp miso paste
2 litres chicken stock
1 litre water
2 tbsp soy sauce
1 tbsp fish sauce
50g shiitake mushrooms, sliced
200g ramen noodles
2 cups leftover turkey meat, shredded
2 cups green cabbage, shredded
2 zucchini, julienned
2 tbsp black & white sesame seeds
1 fresh green chilli
2 sheets nori

Makes *4 serves*
Takes *1 hour*

Dairy-free

Method

Place turkey carcass/bones, pan juices, the whites of the spring onions (reserve the greens for garnish), ginger, garlic, miso paste, chicken stock and water into a large saucepan and bring to a boil. Reduce heat and simmer, skimming occasionally, for 45 minutes, until slightly reduced.

Strain soup into a clean pot, and add soy sauce and fish sauce. Return to a simmer, add mushrooms and cook for 4–5 minutes, until tender. Taste, and season with salt and freshly ground black pepper.

Cook noodles according to packet directions, and split evening between 4 bowls. Top with shredded turkey, cabbage, zucchini ribbons and mushrooms.

Toast sesame seeds in a small, dry frying pan over medium heat.

Ladel broth over turkey and noodles and garnish with thinly sliced spring onion, sesame seeds, finely sliced green chilli and squares of nori.

Tip *If you don't feel like souping it, freeze the turkey bones and make this when the weather starts to cool!*

Boxing Day Bubble & Squeak Cakes

I don't know about you, but leftover potatoes are pretty much a given in our household, and come Boxing Day these hash cakes are the perfect way to those tasty morsels a new lease of life with very minimal effort. Whether it's for brunch, lunch or a light dinner, this forgiving recipe will have everyone back at the table for seconds!

Ingredients

2 tbsp olive oil
4 rashers streaky bacon (or leftover Christmas ham), diced
½ cup cabbage, thinly sliced
½ red onion, thinly sliced
4 cups cooked potatoes, roughly diced
1 tbsp capers
1 small handful parsley, roughly chopped
1 egg, beaten
3 tbsp fine polenta, or breadcrumbs

Quick tartare sauce

1 egg yolk
2 cloves garlic, crushed
1 tsp white wine vinegar
1 small lemon, zested & juiced
1 tsp wholegrain mustard
½ cup vegetable oil
3 tbsp capers, drained & chopped
3 tbsp gherkins, drained & chopped
1 small shallot, finely chopped
1 small lemon, zested & juiced
3 tbsp fresh parsley, finely chopped

***Makes** 4 serves*
***Takes** 40 minutes*

Method

Heat the oil in a large frying pan over medium heat. Add the bacon (or ham) and fry until browned. Add cabbage and onion and saute for 1–2 minutes, until softened. Remove the pan from the heat and spoon cabbage mixture into a large bowl.

Add the potatoes, mixing to combine, mashing the potatoes slightly but leaving some chunky. Add the capers, parsley and egg, and season with salt and freshly ground black pepper.

Portion the mixture into evenly-sized patties, flattening each patty with your hands. Coat lightly in polenta, and place in the fridge for 30 minutes, to firm up.

To make the quick tartare sauce, add the egg yolk, garlic, vinegar, 1 tsp of lemon juice and mustard to the small bowl of a food processor. Blend to combine, and then with the food processor still running, slowly add the oil, a few drops at a time, until the oil is incorporated and the mixture has emulsified. Add salt and freshly ground black pepper, adjusting the seasoning as necessary.

When you're ready to cook, return the pan to the heat and add some extra oil, if needed. Fry each bubble & squeak cake for 2–3 minutes on each side, until crispy and browned.

Serve with extra parsley leaves and a decent drizzle of tartare sauce.

Tip There is so much scope to add anything you like to this recipe — leftover roast vegetables, corn, different herbs, salmon or smoked fish, or simply leave them as potato cakes and served topped with a poached egg!

Cook's Note

Make these pies ahead of time and store in an airtight container. You can layer them between sheets of baking paper. To reheat before serving, pop into a warm oven for 4–5 minutes, before dusting with icing sugar.

Christmas Mince Pies

Make your own this Christmas... not only will they be far better than the store-bought ones, but they make excellent gifts. There are several shortcuts you can take — buy sweet shortcrust pastry, and buy pre-made fruit mince — but I've included recipes for both here so you can make them 100% from scratch if you choose. Serve warm with a dusting of icing sugar for the ultimate festive treat.

Ingredients

Fruit mince

1 apple, peeled, cored and finely diced
½ cup sultanas
½ cup mixed peel
½ cup currants
½ cup pistachios, chopped
1 cup soft brown sugar
½ teaspoon ground cinnamon
½ teaspoon mixed spice
¼ teaspoon ground nutmeg
3 tbsp butter, melted
2 tablespoon brandy
1 lemon, zested & juiced
1 orange, zested & juiced

Pastry

2 cup flour
2 tbsp almond meal
180g cold butter, chopped
¼ cup icing sugar
1 egg yolk
¼ cup milk
1 egg, lightly beaten

Makes *36 pies*
Takes *60 minutes*

Method

Make the fruit mince in advance. Place all of the ingredients into a large saucepan and bring to a gentle simmer over low heat. Cook for 20 minutes, until the fruit has broken down and absorbed most of the liquid. Remove from the heat and allow to cool a little, before spooning into sterlilised jars and storing in the fridge for up to 2 weeks.

To make the pastry, sift flour into a large bowl and then stir in almond meal. Rub in the butter with your fingers. Sift in icing sugar. Make a well in the centre of the bowl and stir in the egg yolk and just enough milk to bring the ingredients together.

On a lightly-floured bench, knead the dough for 4–5 minutes, until smooth. Cover with cling film and refrigerate for 30 minutes.

Preheat oven to 180°C.

Roll out pastry to 3mm thickness, and cut out 7.5cm rounds. Press into pre-greased shallow round patty pans. Drop tablespoons of fruit mince into each hole. Re-roll the pastry scraps and cut into different shapes. Brush each shape with beaten egg and place egg-side down on top of the fruit mince.

Bake for 15–20 minutes or until lightly browned. Transfer to a baking rack and allow to cool slightly.

Dust with icing sugar just before serving.

Find it

A

almonds
  Olive oil & sea salt muesli 84
  Persian rice salad 141
  Pesto — three ways 40
  Amit's flatbreads 209
anchovies
  Café de Paris butter 35
  Rocket & caper dressing 225
apples
  Fruit mince 257
  Korean beef short rib tacos (salsa) 159
asparagus: One-hour focaccia 95
avocados
  Beetroot, citrus & avocado salad 137
  Spinach, smoked salmon & avocado pizza 72

B

bacon
  Bacon caramel 61
  Bacon, walnut & roasted radish salad 133
  Boxing Day bubble and squeak cakes 254
  One skillet breakfast frittata 66
basil
  Lighter tomato & tuna Niçoise salad 138
  One-hour focaccia 95
  Orange, caper & basil salsa 43
  Pesto — three ways 40
  A zillion herbs butterflied chicken 239
bean sprouts
  Beef brisket bibimbap bowl 176
  Thai green chicken curry 149
beans, black
  Huevos rancheros breakfast pizza 72
  Mexican beef and black bean meatballs 156
beans, green
  JB's fish larb 145
  Lighter tomato & tuna Niçoise salad 138
beef
  Beef brisket bibimbap bowl 176
  Best Bolognese 160
  Corned beef balls 113
  Korean beef short rib tacos 159
  Leftover roast beef sarnie 114
  Mexican beef and black bean meatballs 156
  Mustard-rolled eye fillet with rosemary salt 250
  Paleo shepherd's pie 175
  Sunday roast 185
beetroot
  Beetroot, citrus & avocado salad 137
  Beetroot pickled eggs 98
  Bacon, walnut & roasted radish salad 133
  Beetroot sauerkraut 13
  Beetroot yoghurt dip with pistachios 48
black beans
  Huevos rancheros breakfast pizza 72
  Mexican beef and black bean meatballs 156
Blackberry, sage & goats' cheese jaffle 83
Blue cheese dressing 225
bok choy: Thai green chicken curry 149
Bolognese, best 160
Breakfast Bolognese bowl 77
Boxing Day bubble and squeak cakes 254
Bread & butter pickles 14
Leftover roast beef sarnie 114
Breakfast Bolognese bowl 77
Bring back the corned beef 182
Brining chicken 236
broccolini
Thai green chicken curry 149
Vietnamese caramel salmon 150
Brunch pizza — three ways 72
butters, flavoured 35–36

C

cabbage
  Beetroot sauerkraut 13
  Boxing Day bubble and squeak cakes 254
  Fast slaw 226
  Homemade vegan kimchi 17
  Leftover turkey ramen 253
  Okonomiyake 163
  Café de Paris butter 35
  Campari: Negroni marmalade 65
capers
  Orange, caper & basil salsa 43
  Rocket & caper dressing 225
capsicums
  Harissa dressing 57
  Pesto — three ways 40
  Rainbow Israeli salad 129
caramel, bacon 61
caramelised onions
  Caramelised onion, chorizo & mushroom pizza 72
  Caramelised onions 21
  Easy crostini 105
  Leftover roast beef sarnie 114
carrots

Carrot, goats' cheese & pine nut salad 134
Fast slaw 226
Homemade vegan kimchi 17
JB's fish larb 145
Persian rice salad 141
Pesto — three ways 40
Roasted carrot & orange soup 172
cauliflower: Persian lamb pie 181
cavolo nero
Cavolo crisps 91
Harry's mushroom stroganoff with plenty of greens 153
Pesto — three ways 40
cheese
see also blue cheese; feta; goats' cheese; mascarpone; mozzarella cheese; Parmesan
Pesto — three ways 40
Pot roast & kimchi Reuben 117
cherries: One-hour focaccia 95
chicken
Brining chicken 236
Chicken salt 216
Slow chicken 220
Thai green chicken curry 149
A zillion herbs butterflied chicken 239
chickpeas: Vegan chickpea curry 206
chips, easy oven baked, with chicken salt 216
chocolate
Chocolate self-saucing pudding 168
Orange & chocolate tiramisu 164
chorizo: Caramelised onion, chorizo & mushroom pizza 72
Christmas mince pies 257
chutney, fresh green 198
Cinnamon honey butter 36
Citrus couscous with orange paprika vinaigrette 232
coconut
Lemon & coconut raw balls 167
Olive oil & sea salt muesli 84
coconut cream
Paleo shepherd's pie 175
Vegan chickpea curry 206
coconut milk
JB's fish larb 145
Tamarind & coconut fish curry 202
Thai green chicken curry 149
coriander
Beef brisket bibimbap bowl 176
Fresh coriander sauce 156
Fresh green chutney 198
Green dressing 235
Green whey salad dressing 53
JB's fish larb 145
Mexican beef and black bean meatballs 156
Mexican butter 35
Orange, caper & basil salsa 43
Persian rice salad 141
Pesto — three ways 40
Pot roast & kimchi Reuben 117
Rainbow Israeli salad 129
Thai green chicken curry 149
Thai green curry paste 146
Tropical salsa 246
Vietnamese caramel salmon 150
A zillion herbs butterflied chicken 239
corned beef
Bring back the corned beef 182
Corned beef balls 113
Pot roast & kimchi Reuben 117
couscous: Citrus couscous with orange paprika vinaigrette 232
cranberries, dried: Persian rice salad 141
crème fraîche
Blue cheese dressing 225
One-hour focaccia 95
crostini, easy 105
cucumbers
Cucumber raita 201
Dill cucumber pickles 25
JB's fish larb 145
Rainbow Israeli salad 129
Summer melon & cucumber salad 126
Szechuan cucumber salad 121
currants
Fruit mince 257
Persian rice salad 141
curry leaves
Tamarind & coconut fish curry 202
Vegan chickpea curry 206
Wency's dhal 205

D

daikon: Homemade vegan kimchi 17
dhal, Wency's 205
dill
Dill cucumber pickles 25
Gin & sumac-cured salmon 71
Green whey salad dressing 53
dressings
Blue cheese dressing 225
Grated tomato dressing 39
Green dressing 235
Green whey salad dressing 53
Harissa dressing 57
Japanese sesame dressing 225
Orange paprika vinaigrette 232
Ranch-style dressing 225
Rocket & caper dressing 225
Sundried tomato dressing 225
Tahini dressing 225
Tahini jar dressing 58
Dukkah 219
Dukkah-rubbed Christmas lamb 249

E

edamame, salt & vinegar 88
eggplant: Thai green chicken curry 149
eggs
- Beetroot pickled eggs 98
- Breakfast Bolognese bowl 77
- Caramelised onion, chorizo & mushroom pizza 72
- Huevos rancheros breakfast pizza 72
- One skillet breakfast frittata 66
- Spinach, smoked salmon & avocado pizza 72
- Yorkies 189

F

Fennel, orange & chilli salt 30
feta
- Huevos rancheros breakfast pizza 72
- Mediterranean baked feta 101
- Zucchini ribbon salad with pomegranate 235

filo pastry: Persian lamb pie 181
fish
- see also salmon; tuna
- JB's fish larb 145
- Tamarind & coconut fish curry 202

flatbreads, Amit's 209
focaccia, one-hour 95
Fresh green chutney 198
frittata, one skillet breakfast 66
fruit mince: Christmas mince pies 257

Garlic confit & garlic bread 109
Gin & sumac-cured salmon 71
goats' cheese
- Blackberry, sage & goats' cheese jaffle 83
- Carrot, goats' cheese & pine nut salad 134
- One-hour focaccia 95

grapefruit
- Beetroot, citrus & avocado salad 137
- Negroni marmalade 65
- Grated tomato dressing 39

green curry paste, Thai 146
Green dressing 235
Green sauce 239
Green whey salad dressing 53
greens
- Harry's mushroom stroganoff with plenty of greens 153
- Pesto — three ways 40

H

Haloumi & pineapple skewers, grilled 219
ham
- Boxing Day bubble and squeak cakes 254
- Negroni-glazed ham 243

Harissa dressing 57
- Carrot, goats' cheese & pine nut salad 134

Harry's mushroom stroganoff with plenty of greens 153
hazelnuts
- Dukkah 219
- Pesto — three ways 40

herbs see also names of individual herbs
- Green whey salad dressing 53
- Ranch-style dressing 225
- A zillion herbs butterflied chicken 239

Homemade vanilla extract 54
Homemade vegan kimchi 17
honey: Cinnamon honey butter 36
Huevos rancheros breakfast pizza 72

J

jaffle, blackberry, sage & goats' cheese 83
jalapeño peppers
- Huevos rancheros breakfast pizza 72
- Orange, caper & basil salsa 43

Jamaican jerk salmon with tropical salsa 246
Japanese sesame dressing 225
JB's fish larb 145

K

kale
- Harry's mushroom stroganoff with plenty of greens 153
- Pesto — three ways 40

kimchi
- Beef brisket bibimbap bowl 176
- Homemade vegan kimchi 17
- Pot roast & kimchi Reuben 117
- Korean beef short rib tacos 159

kumara: Paleo shepherd's pie 175

L

Labneh 44
- Marinated labneh balls 102
- Roasted plums with thyme and labneh 78
- Summer melon & cucumber salad 126

lamb
- Dukkah-rubbed Christmas lamb 249
- Persian lamb pie 181

Leftover roast beef sarnie 114
Leftover turkey ramen 253
lemons

Beetroot, citrus & avocado salad 137
Fruit mince 257
Korean beef short rib tacos (salsa) 159
Lemon & coconut raw balls 167
Lemon & sage roasted turkey 240
lentils: Wency's dhal 205
Lighter tomato & tuna Niçoise salad 138
limes
Beetroot, citrus & avocado salad 137
Tropical salsa 246

M

Marinated labneh balls 102
marmalade, Negroni 65
mascarpone: Orange & chocolate tiramisu 164
Mediterranean baked feta 101
Easy crostini 105
melons: Summer melon & cucumber salad 126
Mexican beef and black bean meatballs 156
Mexican butter 35
mint
Citrus couscous with orange paprika vinaigrette 232
Fresh green chutney 198
JB's fish larb 145
Korean beef short rib tacos (salsa) 159
Mint butter 36
Pesto — three ways 40
Tomato kachumber 201
A zillion herbs butterflied chicken 239
mozzarella cheese
Corned beef balls 113
Lighter tomato & tuna Niçoise salad 138
muesli, olive oil & sea salt 84
mushrooms
Caramelised onion, chorizo & mushroom pizza 72
Harry's mushroom stroganoff with plenty of greens 153
Leftover turkey ramen 253
Mustard-rolled eye fillet with rosemary salt 250

N

Nacho popcorn 215
Negroni marmalade 65
Negroni-glazed ham 243
noodles
Beef brisket bibimbap bowl 176
Leftover turkey ramen 253
Vietnamese caramel salmon 150
Nori & sesame butter 36
nuts
see also almonds; hazelnuts; pine nuts; walnuts
Olive oil & sea salt muesli 84
Pesto — three ways 40

O

Okonomiyake 163
olive oil
Garlic confit & garlic bread 109
Marinated labneh balls 102
Olive oil & sea salt muesli 84
Tomato confit 106
Tuna confit 110
olives
Lighter tomato & tuna Niçoise salad 138
Mediterranean baked feta 101
One skillet breakfast frittata 66
One-hour focaccia 95
onions
see also caramelised onions
Bread & butter pickles 14
Bring back the corned beef 182
Harissa dressing 57
oranges
Beetroot, citrus & avocado salad 137
Bring back the corned beef 182
Citrus couscous with orange paprika vinaigrette 232
Easy pickled oranges 26
Fennel, orange & chilli salt 30
Fruit mince 257
Negroni marmalade 65
Orange, caper & basil salsa 43
Orange & chocolate tiramisu 164
Roasted carrot & orange soup 172
Oven baked chips, easy, with chicken salt 216

P

Paleo shepherd's pie 175
Parmesan
Breakfast Bolognese bowl 77
Garlic confit & garlic bread 109
Harry's mushroom stroganoff with plenty of greens 153
Mexican butter 35
One skillet breakfast frittata 66
Pesto — three ways 40
parsley
Café de Paris butter 35
Carrot, goats' cheese & pine nut salad 134
Fast slaw 226
Green dressing 235

Green whey salad dressing 53
Marinated labneh balls 102
Pesto — three ways 40
Rainbow Israeli salad 129
A zillion herbs butterflied chicken 239
Zucchini ribbon salad with pomegranate 235
pasta
Best Bolognese 160
Breakfast Bolognese bowl 77
Harry's mushroom stroganoff with plenty of greens 153
Pear frangipani tart 193
Persian lamb pie 181
Persian rice salad 141
Pesto — three ways 40
pine nuts
Carrot, goats' cheese & pine nut salad 134
Pesto — three ways 40
pineapple
Grilled haloumi & pineapple skewers 219
Tropical salsa 246
pistachios
Beetroot yoghurt dip with pistachios 48
Persian rice salad 141
Pesto — three ways 40
pizza: Brunch pizza — three ways 72
plums: Roasted plums with thyme and labneh 78
pomegranate
Persian rice salad 141
Rainbow Israeli salad 129
Zucchini ribbon salad with pomegranate 235
popcorn, nacho 215
Pot roast & kimchi Reuben 117
potatoes
Boxing Day bubble and squeak cakes 254
Corned beef balls 113
Easy oven baked chips with chicken salt 216
Rosemary roast potatoes 186
prawns: Okonomiyake 163
prosciutto: Easy crostini 105
pumpkin seeds: Olive oil & sea salt muesli 84

R

radishes
Bacon, walnut & roasted radish salad 133
Korean beef short rib tacos (salsa) 159
Rainbow Israeli salad 129
Rainbow Israeli salad 129
raisins
Olive oil & sea salt muesli 84
Persian rice salad 141
ramen noodles: Leftover turkey ramen 253
Ranch-style dressing 225
Reuben sandwich, Pot roast & kimchi 117
rice
JB's fish larb 145
Persian rice salad 141
rocket
Pesto — three ways 40
Rocket & caper dressing 225
rolled oats: Olive oil & sea salt muesli 84
Rosemary roast potatoes 186
Rosemary salt 250

S

sage
Blackberry, sage & goats' cheese jaffle 83
Lemon & sage roasted turkey 240
salad leaves
Bacon, walnut & roasted radish salad 133
JB's fish larb 145
Leftover roast beef sarnie 114
Lighter tomato & tuna Niçoise salad 138
salmon
Gin & sumac-cured salmon 71
Jamaican jerk salmon with tropical salsa 246
Spinach, smoked salmon & avocado pizza 72
Vietnamese caramel salmon 150
Salt & vinegar edamame 88
salts, flavoured
Chicken salt 216
Fennel, orange and chilli salt 30
Rosemary salt 250
sandwiches
Leftover roast beef sarnie 114
Pot roast & kimchi Reuben 117
sauerkraut, beetroot 13
savoiardi (ladyfinger) biscuits: Orange & chocolate tiramisu 164
sesame seeds
Dukkah 219
Leftover turkey ramen 253
Nori & sesame butter 36
Olive oil & sea salt muesli 84
Persian rice salad 141
shepherd's pie, paleo 175
slaw, fast 226
Slow chicken 220
soup
Leftover turkey ramen 253
Roasted carrot & orange soup 172
spinach
Green dressing 235
One skillet breakfast frittata 66
Persian lamb pie 181
Spinach, smoked salmon &

  avocado pizza 72
  A zillion herbs butterflied chicken 239
spring onions
  Korean beef short rib tacos (salsa) 159
  One-hour focaccia 95
  Vietnamese caramel salmon 150
sultanas
  Fruit mince 257
  Persian rice salad 141
sumac
  Gin & sumac-cured salmon 71
  Rainbow Israeli salad 129
  Summer melon & cucumber salad 126
  Sunday roast 185
  Sundried tomato dressing 225
sunflower seeds: Olive oil & sea salt muesli 84
sweets
  Chocolate self-saucing pudding 168
  Christmas mince pies 257
  Lemon & coconut raw balls 167
  Orange & chocolate tiramisu 164
  Pear frangipani tart 193
Szechuan peppercorns
  Szechuan cucumber salad 121
  Szechuan oil 122

T

tacos, Korean beef short rib 159
Tahini dressing 225
Tahini jar dressing 58
  Beetroot, citrus & avocado salad 137
Tamarind & coconut fish curry 202
Thai green chicken curry 149
Thai green curry paste 146
thyme: Roasted plums with thyme and labneh 78
tiramisu, orange & chocolate 164
tomatoes
  Grated tomato dressing 39
  Grilled haloumi & pineapple skewers 219
  Huevos rancheros breakfast pizza 72
  Lighter tomato & tuna Niçoise salad 138
  Mediterranean baked feta 101
  One skillet breakfast frittata 66
  Rainbow Israeli salad 129
  Tomato confit 106
  Tomato kachumber 201
tomatoes, canned
  Best Bolognese 160
  Mexican beef and black bean meatballs 156
  Paleo shepherd's pie 175
  Tamarind & coconut fish curry 202
  Vegan chickpea curry 206
tomatoes, sundried
  Pesto — three ways 40
  Sundried tomato dressing 225
  Tropical salsa 246
tuna
  Lighter tomato & tuna Niçoise salad 138
  Tuna confit 110
turkey
  Leftover turkey ramen 253
  Lemon & sage roasted turkey 240

vanilla extract, homemade 54
Vegan chickpea curry 206
Vietnamese caramel salmon 150
vodka: Homemade vanilla extract 54

walnuts
  Bacon, walnut & roasted radish salad 133
  Pesto — three ways 40
Wedge salad favourites 225
Wency's dhal 205
whey: Green whey salad dressing 53

yoghurt
  Amit's flatbreads 209
  Beetroot yoghurt dip with pistachios 48
  Cucumber raita 201
  Fresh green chutney 198
  Labneh 44
  Persian lamb pie 181
Yorkies 189

Z

Za'atar spice mix 126
A zillion herbs butterflied chicken 239
zucchini
  Bread & butter pickles 14
  Leftover turkey ramen 253
  Tropical salsa 246
  Zucchini ribbon salad with pomegranate 235

Dream Team

It takes a lot of moving parts and helping hands to write, shoot and edit a cookbook, whilst simultaneously running a business. The chefs are up before dawn, baking scones, building sandwiches and tossing salads to fill the delis before the first coffee is poured. The drivers are filling the JUK trucks and zipping from suburb to suburb, delivering tasty parcels of homemade meals to our customers. The office team are answering phones, replying to emails and managing their teams — no day is ever the same! I couldn't have done this without a giant JUK support network. There are too many superstars to name in one go, but special thanks goes to:

Lottie Hedley — *for always finding 'the shot' and for her endless patience*

Jess Brewer — *for wearing no less than 100 hats at a time*

Harry Tickler — *the best sous chef a gal could ask for*

Jenny Moore — *for dotting the i's and crossing the t's*

Jono Brooker — *for coming home with wine when I need it most*

The JUK team — *an incredibly close-knit group of superstars who make me proud on the daily*

Our customers — *for letting us feed you every day, for believing in our dream and for your unwavering support*

Thank you!